FIVE
POWER
DEFENCE
ARRANGEMENTS
AT FORTY

The **S. Rajaratnam School of International Studies (RSIS)** was officially inaugurated on 1 January 2007. Before that, it was known as the Institute of Defence and Strategic Studies (IDSS), which was established ten years earlier on 30 July 1996. Like its predecessor, RSIS was established as an autonomous entity within the Nanyang Technological University (NTU).

The School exists to develop a community of scholars and policy analysts at the forefront of Asia Pacific security studies and international affairs. Its three core functions are research, graduate teaching and networking activities in the Asia-Pacific region. It produces cutting-edge security related research in Asia Pacific Security, Conflict and Non-Traditional Security, International Political Economy, and Country and Area Studies.

The School's activities are aimed at assisting policymakers to develop comprehensive approaches to strategic thinking on issues related to security and stability in the Asia Pacific and their implications for Singapore.

For more information about RSIS, please visit <http://www.rsis.edu.sg/>.

The **Institute of Southeast Asian Studies (ISEAS)** was established as an autonomous organization in 1968. It is a regional centre dedicated to the study of socio-political, security and economic trends and developments in Southeast Asia and its wider geostrategic and economic environment. The Institute's research programmes are the Regional Economic Studies (RES, including ASEAN and APEC), Regional Strategic and Political Studies (RSPS), and Regional Social and Cultural Studies (RSCS).

ISEAS Publishing, an established academic press, has issued more than 2,000 books and journals. It is the largest scholarly publisher of research about Southeast Asia from within the region. ISEAS Publishing works with many other academic and trade publishers and distributors to disseminate important research and analyses from and about Southeast Asia to the rest of the world.

FIVE POWER
DEFENCE ARRANGEMENTS AT FORTY

EDITED BY

IAN STOREY
RALF EMMERS
DALJIT SINGH

S. RAJARATNAM SCHOOL
OF INTERNATIONAL STUDIES
A Graduate School of Nanyang Technological University

PONDER THE IMPROBABLE

ISEAS

INSTITUTE OF SOUTHEAST ASIAN STUDIES
Singapore

First published in Singapore in 2011 by ISEAS Publishing
Institute of Southeast Asian Studies
30 Heng Mui Keng Terrace
Pasir Panjang
Singapore 119614

E-mail: publish@iseas.edu.sg
Website: <http://bookshop.iseas.edu.sg>

The responsibility for facts and opinions in this publication rests exclusively with the authors and their interpretations do not necessarily reflect the views or the policy of the publisher or its supporters.

ISEAS Library Cataloguing-in-Publication Data

The Five Power Defence Arrangements at forty / edited by Ian Storey, Ralf
  Emmers and Daljit Singh.
  "This volume has its genesis in a conference co-organized by the S. Rajaratnam
  School of International Studies (RSIS) and Institute of Southeast Asian Studies
  (ISEAS) in March 2011"—Foreword.
  1. Five Power Defence Arrangements—Congresses.
  2. National security—Asia—Congresses.
  3. Asia—Defenses—Congresses.
  4. Military assistance—Congresses.
  I. Storey, Ian, 1970–
  II. Emmers, Ralf.
  III. Daljit Singh.
  IV. S. Rajaratnam School of International Studies.
  V. Institute of Southeast Asian Studies.
  VI. Conference on the Five Power Defence Arrangements at Forty (2011 :
      Singapore)
UA830 F56   2011

ISBN 978-981-4345-44-6 (hard cover)
ISBN 978-981-4345-40-8 (eBook, PDF)

Typeset by Superskill Graphics Pte Ltd
Printed in Singapore by

Contents

Contributors

Ang Cheng Guan is Associate Professor and Head, Humanities and Social Studies Education Academic Group of the National Institute of Education (HSSE/NIE) and Adjunct Senior Fellow of the S. Rajaratnam School of International Studies (RSIS), Singapore. He is the author of *Vietnamese Communist Relations with China and the Second Indo-China Conflict, 1956–1962* (MacFarland, 1997), *The Vietnam War from the Other Side: The Vietnamese Communists' Perspective* (RoutledgeCurzon, 2002), *Ending the Vietnam War: The Vietnamese Communists' Perspective* (Routledge Curzon, 2004) and *Southeast Asia and the Vietnam War* (Routledge, 2010).

Sam Bateman is a Senior Fellow and adviser to the Maritime Security Programme at the S. Rajaratnam School of International Studies (RSIS) at the Nanyang Technological University (NTU) in Singapore. He is a former officer in the Royal Australian Navy who became the first Director of the Centre for Maritime Policy (now the Australian National Centre for Ocean Resources and Security) at the University of Wollongong. He remains an adjunct Professorial Research Fellow of that Centre. He has written extensively on defence and maritime issues in Australia, the Asia Pacific and the Indian Ocean.

Ralf Emmers is Associate Professor and Acting Head of the Centre for Non-Traditional Security Studies at the S. Rajaratnam School of International Studies (RSIS), Nanyang Technological University (NTU), Singapore. He is the author of *Geopolitics and Maritime Territorial Disputes in East Asia* (Routledge, 2010), *Non-Traditional Security in the Asia-Pacific: The Dynamics of Securitization* (Marshall Cavendish, 2004), *Cooperative Security and the Balance of Power in ASEAN and the ARF* (RoutledgeCurzon, 2003), and the co-author of *The East Asia Summit and the Regional Security Architecture*

(University of Maryland School of Law, 2011). Ralf is also the editor of several edited volumes and has published numerous articles in peer-reviewed journals.

Tim Huxley is Executive Director of The International Institute for Strategic Studies-Asia (IISS), Singapore. Tim has worked for many years in the overlap between strategic studies and Asian area studies, his research focusing particularly on the security and defence policies of Southeast Asian states. Before joining the IISS in 2003, he was Reader in South-East Asian Politics and Director of the Centre for South-East Asian Studies at the University of Hull, England. He is the author of *Defending the Lion City: The Armed Forces of Singapore* (Allen & Unwin, 2000). He became Executive Director of IISS-Asia in 2007.

Jim Rolfe is the Deputy Director of the Asia Pacific Civil Military Centre of Excellence in Canberra, Australia. Previously he has been Associate Professor of International Relations at the Asia-Pacific Center for Security Studies in Hawaii, Deputy Director of the New Zealand Centre for Strategic Studies and Associate Director of the Master of International Relations programme at Victoria University of Wellington, New Zealand. Earlier still, following a career in the New Zealand Army, Jim was a policy adviser in the New Zealand Department of the Prime Minister and Cabinet.

Mark G. Rolls is a Senior Lecturer and Co-Director of the International Relations and Security Studies Programme at the University of Waikato, New Zealand. He is the co-editor of *Post-Cold War Security Issues in the Asia-Pacific Region* (Frank Cass, 1994, 2000) and the author of *The Arms Dynamic in South East Asia during the Second Cold War* (Ashgate, 2002). Mark is a regular participant for New Zealand in the Track II process of political, economic and security dialogue in the Asia-Pacific region. He is a Fellow of the Centre for Strategic Studies, New Zealand.

Johan Saravanamuttu is Visiting Senior Research Fellow at the Institute of Southeast Asian Studies (ISEAS), Singapore and was formerly professor of political science at Universiti Sains Malaysia (USM) in Penang where he served as Dean of the School of Social Sciences (1994–96). In 1997, he was the Visiting Chair in ASEAN and International Studies at the University of Toronto. His recent books are *Malaysia's Foreign Policy, the First 50 Years:*

Alignment, Neutralism, Islamism (ISEAS, 2010), *Islam and Politics in Southeast Asia* (Routledge, 2010) and *New Politics in Malaysia*, (ISEAS, 2003).

Daljit Singh, a Visiting Senior Research Fellow at the Institute of Southeast Asian Studies (ISEAS), is an experienced observer of the regional security scene, first from the vantage point of senior appointments in the Singapore public service in his earlier career, including in the Ministry of Defence, and then as a scholar at ISEAS. His current research interests include the major powers in Southeast Asian security, regional security architecture and terrorism. He has edited or co-edited several books on security-related subjects, written book chapters and articles and contributed opinion pieces in the local and international press. He is also the editor of *Southeast Asian Affairs*, the annual review of Southeast Asia published by ISEAS.

Ian Storey is Senior Fellow at the Institute of Southeast Asian Studies (ISEAS), Singapore. Ian's research interests include Southeast Asia's relations with China and the United States, maritime security in the Asia Pacific, and China's foreign and defence policies. Prior to joining ISEAS he held academic positions at the Asia-Pacific Center for Security Studies in Honolulu and at Deakin University in Melbourne. At ISEAS Ian is the editor of the academic journal *Contemporary Southeast Asia*. His latest book is *Southeast Asia and the Rise of China: The Search for Security* (Routledge, 2011).

Carlyle A. Thayer is Emeritus Professor. He joined The University of New South Wales (UNSW) in 1979 and taught at The Royal Military College-Duntroon and then the Australian Defence Force Academy (1985–2010). His career includes appointments to the Asia-Pacific Center for Security Studies in Hawaii (1999–02), The Centre for Defence and Strategic Studies (2002–04) and Australian Command and Staff College (2006–07 and 2010) co-located at the Australian Defence College. He was appointed Distinguished Visiting Professor at Johns Hopkins University (2005) and Ohio University (2008). He is the author of over 400 publications including *Southeast Asia: Patterns of Security Cooperation* (ASPI, 2010).

Geoffrey Till is Emeritus Professor of Maritime Studies at King's College London, Director of the Corbett Centre for Maritime Policy Studies and Visiting Senior Research Fellow at the Defence Studies Department at the

UK Joint Services Command and Staff College. Since 2009 he has also been a Visiting Professor at the S. Rajaratnam School of International Studies (RSIS), Nanyang Technological University (NTU), Singapore. In addition to many articles and chapters on various aspects of maritime strategy and defence policy, he is the author of a number of books including *Seapower: A Guide for the 21st Century* (Routledge, 2nd edition, 2009).

Zakaria Ahmad is Senior Vice President (Research) at HELP University College, Kuala Lumpur, Malaysia. He is also a Distinguished Fellow of the Malaysian Armed Forces Defence College. He received his B.SocSci from the University of Singapore (1970), his Masters degree from McMaster University (1971) and his PhD from the Massachusetts Institute of Technology (1977). He has published extensively on public and international affairs of Malaysia, ASEAN and Pacific Asia. He previously taught at the Science University of Malaysia, University of Malaya, Universiti Kebangsaan Malaysia and was the Tun Razak Chair at Ohio University (2000–03).

Foreword

This volume has its genesis in a conference co-organized by the S. Rajaratnam School of International Studies (RSIS) and the Institute of Southeast Asian Studies (ISEAS) in March 2011 entitled the "Five Power Defence Arrangements at Forty". The conference celebrated the FPDA's contribution to regional security over the last four decades and explored its response to changes in the strategic environment.

The FPDA was set up in 1971 at a time of considerable geopolitical uncertainty. It was not just Singapore-Malaysian relations that were touchy at the time, after the Separation of 1965. The Association of Southeast Asian Nations (ASEAN) was also new, having been established only a few years earlier, and its members were still in the early stages of building confidence to work together to face the common security challenge of the time, namely communism. The war in Vietnam was not going well for the non-communist side, and a US withdrawal seemed inevitable at some point. US President Richard Nixon had already announced the Guam Doctrine in 1969, according to which American involvement in wars on the Asian mainland would be limited to a supportive role while allies and friends would be expected to bear the main burden of defending themselves by providing ground troops.

In 1971, nobody could tell how long the FPDA would last. Sceptics dismissed it as an impotent successor to the Anglo-Malaysian Defence Agreement (AMDA), a mere figleaf to cover the British military withdrawal from the region. They were proved wrong, given the fact that it has lasted 40 years and its five members continue to attest to its ongoing relevance. It has proved to be a valuable confidence-maintaining mechanism and its built-in flexibility allows it to adapt to a changing security environment.

Since its inception in 1971, the FPDA has played a critical confidence-building role in Singapore-Malaysian relations. Before its formation, the Malaysian and Singaporean armed forces had long been comfortable with working with British, Australian and New Zealand forces. Despite some difficulties in bilateral ties, the close defence cooperation has been sustained over the years through the FPDA and its military exercises. Rather than deliberately examining Malaysia and Singapore as two separate strategic entities, the FPDA has worked on the premise that pursuing the security of one nation separately of the other would be counter-productive. The late Professor Michael Leifer forcefully argued that the Arrangements were precisely "predicated on the indivisibility of the defence" of the two Southeast Asian nations.

Furthermore, the FPDA has provided Singapore and Malaysia with a useful avenue to maintain and deepen strong defence ties with Australia, the United Kingdom and New Zealand. Singapore, in particular, has sought to cultivate relations with external powers with the aim of deepening their benign involvement in Southeast Asian security. The FPDA has played such a "cultivating" role.

The complexity and scope of the FPDA exercised have been significantly expanded over the years to address a series of new challenges, ranging from maritime security to humanitarian assistance and disaster relief. The combined exercises have enabled the five powers to enhance professionalism, personal relationships, capacity building and interoperability. The exercises are designed to enhance the capability of the five powers to plan and execute complex multi-national operations. Through its combined annual exercises the FPDA provides a form of military collaboration absent from other regional cooperative arrangements.

Today we are again facing geopolitical uncertainty arising from shifting power balances and various territorial disputes, especially in the maritime domain. There are also a host of non-traditional security threats to address. Compared to 1971, there are more cooperative security mechanisms available to tackle these issues, mostly centred around ASEAN and ASEAN-led institutions. Nevertheless, the FPDA at 40 remains a valuable component of the overall security architecture at a time of change and uncertainty. We trust that the FPDA will continue to play an important role in Southeast Asian security, as long as it preserves its inherent flexibility and consultative nature.

K. Kesavapany
Director, Institute of Southeast Asian Studies (ISEAS), Singapore

Barry Desker
Dean, S. Rajaratnam School of International Studies (RSIS),
Nanyang Technological University (NTU), Singapore

Glossary

AAW	anti-air warfare
ADB	Asian Development Bank
ADEX	Air Defence Exercises
ADF	Australian Defence Force
ADMM-Plus	ASEAN Defence Ministers' Meeting Plus
AMDA	Anglo-Malayan Defence Agreement/Anglo-Malaysian Defence Agreement
ANZAM	Anglo-New Zealand-Australia-Malaya Agreement
ANZUK	Australia-New Zealand-United Kingdom
AOC	Air Officer Commanding
ARF	ASEAN Regional Forum
ASEAN	Association of Southeast Asian Nations
ASW	anti-submarine warfare
ASUW	anti-surface warfare
CBM	confidence-building measure
CPEX	Command Planning Exercise
DRR	Disaster Risk Reduction
EEZ	exclusive economic zone
GMP	Global Maritime Partnership
HA/DR	Humanitarian Assistance and Disaster Relief
IADS	Integrated Air Defence System/Integrated Area Defence System
ICJ	International Court of Justice
IFC	Information Fusion Centre
IMO	International Maritime Organization
ISC	Information Sharing Centre
ISPS	International Ship and Port Security
JCC	Joint Consultative Council
MDA	maritime domain awareness

MOEC	Multinational Operations and Exercise Centre
MOOTW	Military Operations Other Than War
MPA	Maritime and Port Authority
MSP	Malacca Straits Patrols
NAM	Non-aligned Movement
NATO	North Atlantic Treaty Organization
NTS	non-traditional security
NZDF	New Zealand Defence Force
PAS	Islamic Party of Malaysia
PCG	Police Coast Guard
PKO	peacekeeping operations
PSI	Proliferation Security Initiative
RAAF	Royal Australian Air Force
RAN	Royal Australian Navy
ReCAAP	Regional Cooperation Agreement on Combating Piracy and Armed Robbery against Ships in Asia
RIMPAC	Rim of the Pacific
RMAF	Royal Malaysian Armed Forces
RMSI	Regional Maritime Security Initiative
RN	Royal Navy
RNZAF	Royal New Zealand Air Force
RNZN	Royal New Zealand Navy
RSN	Republic of Singapore Navy
SAF	Singapore Armed Forces
SEACAT	Southeast Asia Cooperation Against Terrorism
SEANWFZ	Southeast Asian Nuclear Weapon-Free Zone
SEATO	South-East Asia Treaty Organization
SLOCs	sea lines of communication
SMSC	Singapore Maritime Security Centre
UK	United Kingdom
UMNO	United Malays National Organization
WMD	weapons of mass destruction
WPNS	Western Pacific Naval Symposium
ZOPFAN	Zone of Peace, Freedom and Neutrality

Introduction

Ian Storey, Ralf Emmers and Daljit Singh

On 2 March 2011, the Institute of Southeast Asian Studies (ISEAS) and the S. Rajaratnam School of International Studies (RSIS) convened a joint conference in Singapore to mark the fortieth anniversary of the Five Power Defence Arrangements (FPDA), the military pact linking two Southeast Asian countries, Singapore and Malaysia, with three external powers, the United Kingdom (UK), Australia and New Zealand. The conference, which was attended by regional and international scholars, senior security practitioners, diplomats and journalists, had three aims: to examine the origins of the FPDA and especially the primary motivations of the five powers; to assess the FPDA's contribution to regional security over the past four decades; and to explore possible future roles for the alliance in the context of emerging geopolitical trends and security challenges in the twenty-first century.

While the speakers offered varied assessments of the origins, utility and future of the FPDA, a consensus emerged on the following points. First, the FPDA's flexibility and adaptability to changes in Asia's security environment over the past 40 years remains its core strength. Second, the FPDA has functioned as an important confidence-building measure (CBM) between Singapore and Malaysia and that it continues to facilitate interoperability, professionalization and cooperation among the armed forces of the five countries. Third, that there is neither a compelling strategic rationale, nor a political desire either within or outside the FPDA, to expand its membership beyond the current five members. Fourth, regional perceptions of the FPDA are generally positive because the Arrangements are not seen as directed against a third party.

The FPDA superseded the 1957 Anglo-Malayan Defence Agreement (AMDA) in 1971. The origins of the alliance lay in the British Labour government's announcement in 1967 that it intended to withdraw its military presence "East of Suez" due to financial difficulties. In 1970 the newly-elected Conservative government decided to maintain some military engagement in the region by proposing a successor to AMDA which would take the form of a "loose consultative political framework".[1] Consequently, the defence ministers of Australia, Malaysia, New Zealand, Singapore and the UK concluded the formation of the FPDA in London on 16 April 1971. On 1 September 1971, the Integrated Air Defence System (IADS) was established within the FPDA framework to safeguard the air defence of the Southeast Asian states. The FPDA formally entered into force the day after the AMDA ceased to exist on 31 October 1971.

The commitments undertaken by the FPDA were restricted to mere consultations and should thus be distinguished from the ones formerly provided by the AMDA. In contrast to its predecessor, the FPDA simply linked the security of the two Southeast Asian nations to a loose and consultative defence arrangement with Britain, Australia and New Zealand, and did not provide concrete security guarantees. In particular, the automatic commitment to respond to an external attack under the AMDA was substituted under the FPDA by an obligation to consult in such an event.[2] Furthermore, the FPDA did not include a commitment to station troops in Malaysia and Singapore.

Nonetheless, despite the absence of clear military commitments, analysts have often referred to the political and psychological deterrence provided by the FPDA to Singapore and Malaysia. The formation of the FPDA followed Indonesian President Sukarno's opposition to the formation of the Federation of Malaysia in September 1963. And despite the establishment of the Association of Southeast Asian Nations (ASEAN) in August 1967, relations with Jakarta continued to be characterized by mistrust. Indonesia was therefore a clear referent of the FPDA when it was first established.

Beyond offering some form of psychological deterrence, the FPDA was also expected to play a confidence-building role in Singapore-Malaysian relations. Singapore's traumatic separation from the Federation of Malaysia in 1965 continued to affect its ties with Kuala Lumpur and the city-state perceived the FPDA as an additional means to regulate its relations with its immediate neighbour.

The structure and activities of the FPDA remained limited in the 1970s and 1980s. The Joint Consultative Council (JCC) was initially established to act as a senior consultative group, bringing together senior officials from the Ministries of Defence of Malaysia and Singapore as well as the High Commissioners of Australia, New Zealand and the UK. The FPDA was organized around a regular series of combined but limited exercises. Its central operational structure was the IADS, located at the Royal Malaysian Air Force Base Butterworth in Malaysia, and put under an Australian commander and the supervision of an Air Defence Council. However, the FPDA remained under-institutionalized during most of the Cold War period.

The role of the FPDA has been strengthened since the end of the Cold War.[3] The FPDA has, since the late 1980s, gradually deepened and broadened its institutional structures and activities. In 1988, it was decided that the FPDA Defence Ministers' Meeting would be held every three years while the FPDA Chiefs' Conference would meet more regularly. The latter have coincided since 2001 with the annual International Institute for Strategic Studies' (IISS) Asia Security Conference (better known as the Shangri-La Dialogue) held annually in Singapore. The IADS was upgraded into the Integrated Area Defence System, integrating air, naval and land forces, with its headquarters in Butterworth in the late 1990s. These institutional transformations have been matched by more sophisticated and encompassing military exercises ranging from maritime security to military preparedness and humanitarian assistance and disaster relief.

This volume contains nine perspectives on the establishment, development and possible future contributions to regional security of the Five Power Defence Arrangements. Geoffrey Till examines the establishment of the FPDA in his chapter but predominately from a British perspective. According to Till, Britain wanted to formalize defence cooperation among the five countries for five reasons: first, to play a continuing defence role in Southeast Asia; second, to provide support to regional Commonwealth members; third, to contain the threat posed by communism; fourth, to support US policy in the Far East; and finally, to protect its economic interests in the region. Till identifies the obstacles that stood in the way of the FPDA's formation, including differences between Malaysia and Singapore, wariness in Australia and New Zealand concerning the resources that would be required to contribute to a multilateral security arrangement, and disillusionment in the UK over the Commonwealth and the "lure of Europe". Till describes how these obstacles were eventually overcome and highlights the successes of the FPDA. These include the easing of frictions between Malaysia and Singapore, contributing to the defeat of communism in Southeast Asia, and enabling the five countries to maintain and expand defence cooperation. Till concludes by noting that it remains unclear at this point how the defence cuts announced in 2010 will impact the UK's ability to contribute to FPDA exercises in the future.

In his chapter, Ang Cheng Guan re-visits the circumstances under which the FPDA was established by examining in detail the 15-month period leading up to its formation in October 1971. Ang describes how the UK was keen to forge new arrangements in Southeast Asia in the light of its financial difficulties and its review of the East of Suez policy. In April 1970, Secretary of State for Defence Denis Healey disclosed that the British government had proposed a new five-power framework to replace AMDA and that he hoped that formal talks could start soon. A newly-elected Conservative government subsequently engaged in a consultative exercise with Canberra, Wellington, Singapore and Kuala Lumpur concerning its future contribution to Commonwealth defence arrangements for the region. The consultations paved the way for more detailed discussions on basing, training and rental issues. After the five parties had met in London in April 1971, Ang observes that the remaining unfinished business involved the negotiations with Malaysia and Singapore on the Annexes. With the Malaysians, the British spent much time discussing the Jungle Warfare Centre whereas with the Singaporeans the issue was over rent and training facilities. As Ang notes these discussions sometimes proved difficult, but all outstanding issues were eventually resolved, paving the way for the FPDA to come into force on 1 November 1971.

Johan Saravanamuttu examines the FPDA in the context of changes in Malaysia's defence and foreign policies after the end of AMDA in 1971. He also touches on the earlier domestic debate in Malaysia over the AMDA, in the process highlighting the important dimension of domestic sensitivities to alliances with Western powers. The author implies that the same sensitivities would prevail today. He sees the FPDA as one instrument in the more flexible and multi-faceted foreign and security policies of Malaysia since 1971, with its loose consultative character enabling it to synchronise well with these policies. The FPDA will continue to be useful as a confidence-building measure between Singapore and Malaysia, for maintaining historic Commonwealth ties and in meeting the broad security needs of Malaysia. However, Saravanamuttu ends on a note of caution: in the changing strategic circumstances of Southeast Asia it is not clear how much importance it will be accorded by the main participating countries in the future. He also flags some "unresolved thorny issues", among them whether the FPDA should cover East Malaysia, whether other ASEAN members should be included and how the FPDA should relate to other ASEAN states like Indonesia.

In his chapter, Carlyle Thayer shows how FPDA exercises have become progressively more complex and sophisticated over the years and outlines the benefits that the FPDA provides to each member country. Thayer sees the FPDA as a credible deterrent in conventional military terms in the rapidly changing security environment in Southeast Asia, even as it has recently developed military capacities to deal with non-conventional or non-traditional threats. The FPDA's move towards complex combined joint exercises coupled with the upgrading of the IADS command and control means that the armed forces of the five states can effectively operate under a single command. Thayer concludes that the FPDA thus plays more than a limited role in its contribution to regional security, particularly through the development of the conventional capabilities of Malaysia and Singapore, both strategically located on choke points on vital waterways linking the Indian and Pacific oceans, and of interoperability between them and Australia, New Zealand and Britain.

Sam Bateman traces the evolution of the FPDA to an increasing focus on the maritime dimensions in recent years because of the greater salience of non-traditional security threats in the maritime domain, especially after 9/11, and the rise of Asian naval powers whose strategic competition is likely to be played out in the maritime theatre, including in the seas in and around Southeast Asia. However, Bateman posits that the value of FPDA has declined in recent years. Two of its members, the UK and New Zealand, now have significantly reduced military capabilities, while Canberra's most important security relationship in Southeast Asia is now with Indonesia which raises the question whether Australia can contribute to a significant contingency involving the FPDA in the Straits of Malacca and the southern part of the South China Sea without Indonesian participation or approval, bearing in mind Jakarta's sensitivities on territorial and archipelagic waters. Meanwhile, Malaysia and Singapore have developed cooperation outside the scope of the FPDA, with Indonesia and Thailand, for providing security in the Straits of Malacca. Further, both countries now have other opportunities for developing their military professionalism, for example through participation in maritime exercises and other activities hosted by the United States, thereby depriving the FPDA of its once unique role in this respect. Nevertheless Bateman does not write off the FPDA. It has, he concedes, not "entirely lost its relevance" and still offers some benefits to the participants in different ways and it serves as "an accepted entry point into the defence and security environment of Southeast Asia" for the three non-Southeast Asian states.

In the next chapter Jim Rolfe addresses how the FPDA might approach the issue of Humanitarian Assistance and Disaster Relief (HA/DR). While Rolfe challenges some of the central assumptions regarding the role of the military in the realm of HA/DR, ultimately he recognizes that due to the scale and frequency of natural disasters in the Asia Pacific, regional governments will continue to rely on the armed forces as "first responders" given that they fulfil a valuable role in terms of their ability to mobilize manpower and material support and provide specialist capabilities. Accordingly, he advises that the debate should not be framed in terms of *whether* armed forces should be used in HA/DR operations but *how*. Rolfe goes on to identify the clashes of culture and the disconnects between civilian and military agencies and cautions that FPDA defence ministers should ask themselves a series of searching questions before contemplating a formal role in HA/DR training and operations. These questions include: How and where can the FPDA add value? How will the five countries work together at the operational level? And could other agencies do the job more effectively and cheaply than the armed forces?

Zakaria Ahmad sees the FPDA as of enduring value and a significant factor in the strategic calculations of its three principal partners, namely Malaysia, Singapore and Australia. For Malaysia and Singapore, the FPDA provides a measure of insurance and deterrence in the event of external aggression which cannot be entirely ruled out. While some importance has now been accorded to non-traditional security (NTS) issues, FPDA military exercises continue to reflect largely traditional security concerns. Indeed, there appears to be no consensus within policy circles as to how the FPDA should approach NTS challenges. There have been internal debates within the Malaysian defence community about the FPDA, but its deterrent value is appreciated and it has remained an important consideration in Malaysia's defence planning. Malaysia is also satisfied with the FPDA's relatively low profile and its gradual consolidation.

Mark Rolls examines New Zealand's evolving perceptions of, and attitude towards, the FPDA over the past four decades. His chapter begins by noting Wellington's initial ambivalence and desire to avoid over committing itself to the defence of Singapore and Malaysia when the Arrangements were first mooted, and, thereafter, differences of opinion between the foreign and defence ministries regarding the FPDA's usefulness. However, the salience of NTS threats in the 1990s, and especially in the first decade of the twenty-first century following the terrorist attacks of September 11, 2001, increased New Zealand's interest in, and support for, the FPDA even as successive governments continued to put a premium on Wellington's active participation in multilateral regional institutions. Rolls concludes that in today's uncertain strategic environment, in which governments are faced with an array of complex challenges, the FPDA still has an important role to play in areas such an enhancing maritime security and HA/DR operations.

In the final chapter Tim Huxley ponders the future of the FPDA. He begins by noting the continued importance of the FPDA's unspoken rationales, namely as a hedge against an assertive Indonesia (which although the author concedes is unlikely cannot be ruled out) and as a mechanism to maintain channels of communication between the Singaporean and Malaysian armed forces during periods of tension, and to build strategic trust between the two countries. In surveying threats to stability in the Asia Pacific — ranging from growing rivalry among the Great Powers, changes in the distribution of power, competition over natural resources and the unforeseen challenges of climate change — Huxley concludes, as many other contributors to this volume do, that the FPDA's "proven adaptability" and "non-provocative form of hedging" will guarantee its relevance well into the future.

Notes

[1] Chin Kin Wah, "The Five Power Defence Arrangements: Twenty Years After", *The Pacific Review* 4, no. 3 (1991): 193.
[2] Paragraph 5, Communiqué issued at the conclusion of the Five Power Ministerial Meeting on the External Defence of Malaysia and Singapore, London, 15–16 April 1971.
[3] Andrew T. H. Tan, "The Five Power Defence Arrangements: The Continuing Relevance", *Contemporary Security Policy* 29, no. 2 (2008): 292–95.

1

A Little Ray of Sunshine: Britain, and the Origins of the FPDA — A Retrospective on Objectives, Problems and Solutions

Geoffrey Till

In the 1950s and early 1960s few doubted that the United Kingdom had a world role and the responsibilities that went with it: "In those days, more than a quarter of a century ago", remarked Lord Carrington the British Foreign Secretary, "it seemed clear that we had indeed such a role and must be ready to play it — and the next few years justified the assumption." Across the board of British politics the simple abandonment of existing commitments was considered unthinkable. Even Edward Heath, that arch-European, when in opposition was adamantly opposed to the cuts decided on by the Labour Government in 1966–68.[1]

Moreover, the British had the forces to put their policy into effect. In 1964 when Healey took over as Defence Secretary, there were more land forces East of Suez than there were confronting the Russians in Germany. The Royal Navy thought of itself as a world-wide actor in defence of the British Empire and Commonwealth, not just as a counter to the Soviet

Northern and Baltic fleets, burgeoning as they were. The Royal Navy had major bases in Singapore, Aden, Bahrain and Labuan in Borneo; the Royal Air Force staging posts at Ascension Island and Gan; and the Army maintained garrisons in Malaya, Hong Kong and Borneo.[2]

This did not, however, imply that the British saw themselves simply as wanting to defend the status quo. The British had always maintained the empire on the cheap because they were basically interested in trade, not territory, and were reluctant to assume the burdens of an empire.[3] For this reason, the British relied on consent of a sort. British imperial historians have for years been making the point that the empire rested essentially on such consent. How else could the British "rule" India, a region of 225–250 million people, with just 1,250 senior civil servants and at most 35,000 British troops?[4] With the growth of nationalism, this consent was withdrawn and the British recognized with considerably greater insight than the Dutch or the French that the status quo was unsustainable. And since the 1880s the economic benefits of maintaining the empire had been getting ever more dubious anyway, why should they try? So, the question arises, what were British objectives at the time of the Anglo-Malayan Defence Agreement (AMDA) and the founding of the Five Power Defence Arrangements (FPDA)?[5]

Objectives

First across Britain's political spectrum, few doubted that Britain still had a worthwhile and continuing role to play in the Far East. Moreover, there was enthusiasm for the idea and the establishment of the Commonwealth. Many thought that Britain needed it. As Sir Oliver Franks in the Reith Lectures of 1954 opined "the basic condition for the continuing greatness of Britain is a vigorous Commonwealth"[6] — such thinking came naturally to most Tories. On the left, Jim Callaghan, Labour Party spokesman on Colonial Affairs in the mid-1950s, Chancellor of the Exchequer in the 1960s, then Prime Minister, spoke for his party of the Commonwealth as a vision of economic and security interdependence on a global scale, and an opportunity to put right what they saw as the occasional injustices of the colonial period.[7]

This meant handing back appropriated territories in a reasonable state, institutionally, economically, and in security terms too, for to quote the Member of Parliament (MP) for Hornsea, "independence without security is meaningless".[8] The British wanted to encourage their ex-colonies to be sufficiently prosperous, democratic, and to adopt the Westminster model. Being democratic meant working with the views of properly elected nationalist politicians wherever possible, but they wanted those politicians and their newly independent countries to be secure as well. "Before we fix a date" for a withdrawal, said Denis Healey, "…we must have an idea of what will happen when we go. We must give our diplomacy a chance to construct a different basis for the security of the countries we are leaving."[9]

As far as the British were concerned, the main threat to the security of Southeast Asia was communist insurgency fostered by the Soviet Union and China. In the 1940s and 1950s, and into the early 1960s, this was considered a very serious threat, particularly in Singapore.[10] As far as the Foreign Office was concerned, the aim was to facilitate the emergence of a "neutralized" Southeast Asia that was able to pursue its own destiny without interference by the communist powers or the West.[11] "The primary objective of Western policy in the Far East", reported the Trend Committee in November 1965, "is the political and military containment of Communist China and the preservation of stability."[12] "We should not wish to see", the Trend Committee added in May 1966, "South East Asia submerged in Communism or otherwise reduced to satellite status by Peking."[13] There was therefore clear need for socio-economic assistance in the shape of the Colombo Plan, and more specifically for Singapore and Malaya to work together in mutual support and balance. Through the 1960s and into the 1970s, the perceived threat morphed into a concern for an overt communist assault on peninsula Malaysia coming from Vietnam, Laos and Cambodia, and through Thailand. "Fighting", said Anthony Royle, Under Secretary for Foreign and Commonwealth Affairs in July 1970, "is now taking place in all three countries of Indo-China, bringing great suffering to their peoples and endangering the peace and prosperity of neighbouring countries in the area." He wanted to make clear "the importance which the new British Government attaches to the restoration or preservation of peace, security and stability throughout the South-East Asian area" against the threat from the north.[14]

Here at least the Americans, engaged in the Vietnam War, were wholly supportive and indeed quite insistent, and another important British objective was to maintain good relations with the United States at a time when British prosperity, the health of the so-called "Sterling area" and

Britain's military safety in Europe all depended in large measure on the United States' support. Preoccupied in the 1960s with Japan, the Korean Peninsula, the Philippines, and Vietnam, the US-in-Asia (the priorities did not seem quite the same on the US East Coast) was worried about Indonesia and the whole of Southeast Asia, and wanted the British to manage the Commonwealth and its continuing responsibilities in the area as a means of containing the communist challenge. It was important for the British to be seen to be acting in this way, particularly at a time when under Harold Wilson, "steeped" as he was "in the pacifist traditions of English Nonconformity", with an "outlook [that] had been refined by the anti-armament, anti-jingo passions of the Bevanite Left, refused to follow the Australians and the New Zealanders into the quagmire of the Vietnam War".[15] While dealing with Malaya, Singapore, and Indonesia were independent responsibilities, the British performance was monitored closely and often critically by a United States much less inclined to the spirit of "pragmatism and judicious concession" to ardent nationalists that characterized the British approach.[16] All the same, "it is of the first importance that we should carry them [the Americans] with us in any changes we wish to make in our overseas dispositions".[17]

Conceptions of Need

Until they could hand over responsibility for self-defence to effective and well-trained local forces, the British accepted that they would need the capacity to deal with current and future threats to the security of the area. They were anxious not to pull out so fast that "their stabilizing influence in the Malayan area might be undermined by any hasty withdrawal from Malayan bases".[18] To prevent this, they thought they needed five things. First, the support of Singapore and Malaysia; second the active military support of Australia and New Zealand; third the ability to maintain small cadre forces in the theatre as a Commonwealth strategic reserve which could act as the basis for regeneration of larger forces should these prove necessary; and fourthly, a base area from which this could be done. Singapore, one of the best equipped naval bases in the world, was the obvious candidate for the latter and the AMDA of October 1957 the means to the former. While Prime Minister Tunku Abdul Rahman was entirely supportive, not least because, being freed for the time being of having to maintain his country's external defence, allowed him to focus his resources on internal development, others in his cabinet were not so sure. Nationalists such as Malaysia's Minister of Agriculture Aziz Ishak, and many of the younger generation of Malaysian politicians, were opposed to the continuing presence of the former colonialists in the area.[19] British diplomats were therefore, fifthly, careful about the words they used to justify a continuing presence, and thus infuriated when in 1957 Duncan Sandys sought to assuage worried Australians and New Zealanders that Britain's nuclear forces would cover forces in this area too, an airy assumption that alarmed and annoyed many in Kuala Lumpur.[20] Many in Kuala Lumpur were also very concerned at AMDA's perceived association with the Southeast Asia Treaty Organization (SEATO).

Some Roadblocks

As a review of the problems confronting British policymakers on the East of Suez issue in the 1960s and early 1970s makes clear, these objectives would be hard to achieve. Nor should the domestic imperatives of British politicians be forgotten. Wilson, Heath and all the rest of them were elected by the British public for reasons quite other than the crafting of a sustainable policy east of Suez — and if they did not know that, their MPs certainly did.[21] For them, the priorities were saving money, social welfare and getting re-elected.

First among the roadblocks was a marked disinclination on the part of the locals to work together in a common cause. The difficult relations between Singapore and Kuala Lumpur and concerns about internal security in Singapore were a major impediment in getting local forces to cooperate closely in mutual defence. Indeed there were those on both sides of this argument who saw each other as the main threat. The British also had severe doubts that Singapore could survive without close association with Malaysia. Accordingly the British resorted to their favourite response to such problems, the notion of federation, but once again this did not work as became all too clear in the tense period leading up to the August 1965 break-up. According to Wilson, "Lee [Kuan Yew] was in a desperate state, bursting into tears in front of the television cameras and regretting the break-up. Nevertheless, he determined to make a go of the newly-independent Singapore. There was great anxiety in Whitehall...."[22]

Moreover the Australians and the New Zealanders (the other locals as far as the distant British were concerned) likewise were wary of being left in the lurch by Britain (again, they would say) and suspicious of the idea that they should devote more resources to the defence of Southeast Asia so that the British could do less. This was particularly difficult during the premiership of Gough Whitlam whose, in the words of Lord Carrington, "facile attitudinizing" in being deliberately different from the United Kingdom just to curry favour with Asian locals and whose flirtation with ostentatious neutralism led Australia to pull its forces out of the Commonwealth Brigade in 1973.[23]

This was often coupled with a growing disillusion with the ideals of Commonwealth in the 1960s when relations between Britain and its former colonies, particularly in Africa, were soured by vituperative criticism of Britain's role over Rhodesia.[24] Thus, Lord Carrington again:

> The Commonwealth is tenuous. It collapses — and is most vulnerable to cynics — if one tries to put too much upon it. The cultural sense of unity between Britain and the nations of Western Europe is much more profound, deeper, older, than anything within the Commonwealth, *per se*.[25]

(Paradoxically, the Tunku, angered by the Commonwealth's refusal to back him against Indonesia, felt similarly disillusioned.[26]) In short, more and more of Britain's politicians were beginning to feel that the Commonwealth, though important to Britain, was fundamentally not as important to its prosperity and its security as Europe was.

Increasingly, Britain was being sucked into the momentous affairs of Europe, whether it liked it or not. Partly this was a matter of Britain having to choose where its long-term strategic interest lay — in Europe or outside it. There was another piece in this puzzle too, which General Charles de Gaulle never hesitated to use whenever convenient. Was Britain European or simply an appendage of the United States doing its bidding all over the world, including in Southeast Asia? The arrivals in government of Europeanists like Edward Heath and Lord Carrington in the early 1970s were best seen as part of a general trend. Lord Carrington exemplified this well in a moment of truth, (paradoxically during a visit to Australia):

> Distance, geography and a history which reaches back thorough centuries of shared Euro experience are realities not sentimental abstractions. Despite the affection I had found for Australia, I realized in a more positive way than hitherto that I was and am a European.[27]

In addition to this, Europe's political and especially economic appeal was slowly rising amongst the political classes, but especially in the traditionally imperialist Tory Party. Its leader, Edward Heath who had promised a major review of the Labour Government's policy of cutting Britain's East of Suez commitments, in fact was imbued with the idea that entry into the European Common Market would mean an end to the years of retreat and decline, and would mark the beginning of a new and exciting period that would lead to a substantial re-ordering of the country's strategic interests and priorities.[28]

This had important strategic and military consequences as well as causes. The North Atlantic Treaty Organization (NATO), above all, was an exercise in multinational and collective self-defence in which concessions on national sovereignty and independence needed to be made. Lord Carrington summed it up well: "In the first place", he wrote, "our major defence commitment was contributory — to NATO." Two points emerge from this deadly accurate and concise summary.

First, NATO was the top priority. As Mr Healey, the Secretary for Defence explained at the time, "From the beginning it was clear that any cut in our commitments must come outside rather than inside the European theatre, since our interest in European security was, and will remain, irreducible."[29]

Second, this contributory and agreed approach to defence decision making was quite different from the national independence that had characterized British policy in the days of the empire. When the NATO treaty was signed, it was clear from the start that the overseas interests of the former colonial powers of Europe would *not* be covered by it, and were essentially seen as national problems of no concern to the alliance as such.

This seismic shift in Britain's strategic perspectives was reinforced by a major change in the intrinsic nature of British defence already in train for other reasons. Traditionally, the defence of Britain and its overseas empire had been regarded as a strategic entity, as one unified requirement, because the Royal Navy's command of the seas meant that the far reaches of the empire could often be defended in Europe by naval action (or the threat of it) in the Western approaches. That same command of the sea also meant that reinforcements for usually quite small local garrisons could be shuttled around the world at will. This happy unity of effort was lost in the Second World War, where Britain's perilous position in the European theatre and loss of command of the Mediterranean meant that reinforcements, *if they could be sent at all*, would need to go the long way round by the Cape of

Good Hope. The sad fate of the HMS *Prince of Wales* and HMS *Repulse* and the loss of the Malaya, Singapore and Burma in 1942 were the direct consequence of this fundamental shift in Britain's strategic geometry. After the war, the previous situation was briefly restored, but not for long.

The disastrous Suez campaign of 1956, fought in some measure to defend the strategic mobility so necessary for the maintenance of the empire, contributed to a major loss of British influence in the Middle East. This in turn threatened to make the empire's sea lines of communication much longer and subject to Egyptian consent. The alternative of sending troops and supplies by air was similarly blocked off by its total reliance on overflight permissions by a whole sequence of countries whose cooperation could certainly not be relied on.[30] What made the prospective vulnerability of reinforcements so bad, of course was the independence of India and Pakistan in 1947 since this had already deprived the British of that great well of *local* manpower which had historically been so important in keeping the Empire going, without excessive reliance on British manpower.[31]

An alternative strategic posture would have been a return to a policy of offshore balancing in which small but mobile land, and especially air and naval, forces could be committed to the area but for this they would need bases. The immediate political situation in Aden and what the British thought the dubious political acceptability of British bases in Malaysia and Singapore made the unwisdom of assuming that the British could stay on the mainland of Asian indefinitely crystal clear. Instead there was the idea of withdrawing "to peripheral positions in Australia and in the islands of the Indian and Pacific Oceans".[32] This would also lessen the risk of getting sucked into local disputes which the British could otherwise avoid. The option of opening up a base in Australia, which in many ways would have been the ideal solution to all these difficulties (although as the British Pacific Fleet had discovered in the Second World War, Australia was a long way from anywhere) but the Australians were far from keen.

All this robbed the British of the great advantage of cost-effective strategic mobility which had enabled them for the last several hundred years, to run the empire on the cheap. Taken together, it highlighted the particular and separate costs of commitments East of Suez and polarized Britain's strategic choices. It brought into sharp relief the fact that staying East of Suez was going to be difficult for practical strategic reasons and would require substantial investment at a time when the economic benefits of Empire, such as they were, had completely gone. By this time Southeast

Asia provided only 3 per cent of British trade and under 6 per cent of its investment revenue; but it absorbed 15 per cent of the Defence Budget.[33] Worst still, it posed in the harshest way, the strategic choices that the British might need to make in the nature and composition of their forces.

During the 1960s, with NATO's slow adoption of a strategy of Flexible Response, the British needed to take more and more seriously the prospect of serious conflict on the plains of the Central Front and in the North Atlantic. Strategic concentration shifted, therefore to land–air forces focused on the Soviet Third Shock Army massed along Britain's 80 miles of the Central Front, on the mobile maritime forces needed to contain Soviet adventurism in Europe's frozen Far North and on the naval/air forces needed to defend the home base and reinforcements coming across the Atlantic. If to this heady brew, one adds the uncertainties of deciding what were the implications of the deployment of nuclear weapons throughout the theatre, it is easy to understand why East of Suez requirements should seem so trivial, even at a time when defence spending in the United Kingdom was nearly three times what it is at present.

The distracting requirements of the defence of distant interests seemed increasingly hard to bear. There was a long list of other such irritating military issues to deal with too — Hong Kong, Rhodesia, Belize, Aden, Rhodesia and Kuwait: "we seemed at the time to be needing to fly battalions in all directions at the drop of a hat."[34]

For the Royal Navy, clearly the chief exponent of the expeditionary rather than the continentalist approach to war-fighting, of an East of Suez role as well as a European one for Britain, the choices and the difficulties were particularly acute.[35] For the Admirals, still scarred by the loss of the *Prince of Wales* and *Repulse* and, as ever being content with nothing but the best, the issue boiled down to the necessary provision of air cover for the fleet when it was engaged in global operations anywhere in the world. The loss of the CVA-01 carrier programme in 1966 destroyed this expectation and was a clear indication that further cuts to East of Suez defence resources and the commitments that justified them were on the way.

In the meantime, and despite the humiliating shocks of the 1956 Suez campaign and the loss of self-confidence that that enterprise caused, Britain's expeditionary land, sea, and air forces were in fact still capable of doing a remarkably cost effective job. Kuwait 1961 in particular was a model of sea-based and cost-effective deterrence, although there was retrospective criticism of the battle-worthiness of UK forces landed from *HMS Bulwark* if it had actually come to a fight against the Iraqi regime threatening the country.[36] The 1962 Brunei Revolt also showed that Britain was able and prepared to act in distant places. This was a more serious revolt than is often realized; it initially went well and was supported by Indonesia, but the British response was fast and effective. Two companies of Gurkhas and 300 British troops were air-lifted in, followed by the balance of 2 battalions and the revolt was quickly suppressed.[37]

However, the government in London was well aware of the costs and risks involved in this kind of military interventionism and there was certainly a desire to keep out of regional conflicts if at all possible. Although he was keen for Britain to do its share in defending Southeast Asia against what was seen as the communist threat, Harold Wilson was determined not to get involved in the Vietnam War and the same approach determined a low-key, non-escalatory response to *Konfrontasi*, which providentially worked quite well.[38] Royal Navy ships were ordered to show "all possible restraint" in operations and their rules of engagement stressed the minimum use of force, and even then only in self-defence.[39] This process of restraint was possible only because of Indonesia's similar reluctance to escalate and its preference for a strategy of subversion rather than overt military attack. Yet this self-restraint was also a reflection of the scantiness of British military forces. The Americans, indeed, were concerned that the British would not be able to handle the situation and feared that they might be sucked into a deeper conflict. Moreover, the Americans thought that thwarting Sukarno could make a communist take-over in Indonesia more likely and that this in turn might threaten their base in the Philippines.[40]

Even with this strategy of restraint, however, at a cost something like one to two million pounds a week low-level conflicts like *Konfrontasi* remained expensive for the hard-pressed British to operate.[41] It imposed a particularly heavy burden on the Royal Navy. In addition to the standard naval deployment that was intended to support the troops landed in Borneo, a maritime blockade was imposed in order to interdict Indonesian attempts to use the sea to inject its forces and to supply them. In addition, there were a number of more aggressive planned responses should the situation deteriorate, and some of these particularly *Operations Althorpe* and *Spillikin* would have required the use of 58 out of the Royal Navy's destroyer/frigate fleet of 90.[42]

The end of *Konfrontasi*, which was announced in Bangkok following talks in May and June 1966 between Malaysia's Deputy Prime Minister Tun Abdul Razak and the Indonesian Foreign Minister, Adam Malik, was therefore greeted with considerable relief in London. "This was going to mean a major change in our defence deployment", said Harold Wilson, who had been skeptical about the case for overseas garrisons from the start "and the chance to bring thousands of men home."[43]

The Economic Argument

What made this strategic option so attractive, of course, was the state of the British economy. As Chancellor, Jim Callaghan had been carefully briefed on his arrival at the Treasury in 1964 on just how bad the state of the British economy was; although in retrospect dwarfed by the colossal rates of the 1990s and early 2000s, the scale of borrowing then seemed dreadful and financial meltdown considered imminent. What seemed to be at stake was the future of sterling as a reserve currency. At a time when replacing fixed with floating currency exchange rates was considered economically ruinous across nearly all the spectrum of British politics, devaluation — the d word — was a solution that dared not speak its name. For a start, it would damage the economic prospects of countries like Malaysia and Singapore, which had loyally kept their reserves in sterling. As a result, the Chancellor was urged to "get a grip on public expenditure". Severe cuts across the board, but especially in areas which did not impact on social welfare, which Labour MPs thought central to the prospects of their re-election, were held to be necessary.[44]

Britain's economic problems were further aggravated by poor productivity and the dreadful state of industrial relations, especially the seamen's strike in 1966 which greatly increased speculation against the pound. Continuing speculator attacks, said Callaghan were "like swimming in a heavy seas. As soon as we emerged from the buffeting of one wave, another would hit us before we could catch our breath." The first financial crisis hit in July 1966, but such was the resistance to it, that devaluation followed only on 18 November 1967, eighteen months later.[45]

As far as most of the Labour Party and some of the cabinet were concerned, British defence spending, especially defence spending East of Suez, was considered a prime target for cuts, because it did not seem much related to the defence of Britain in Europe, because local threats in the wake of the end of *Konfrontasi* and the evident survival of Singapore seemed much less acute and because many saw the effort to maintain the commitment as a pointless sop to a failing American policy. When sober, George Brown at the Department of Economic Affairs, was a particularly vociferous and articulate advocate of this line. The Americans, preoccupied with Vietnam, were putting Britain under great pressure to stay East of Suez and there were delicate indications that the extent of American support for sterling in its travails might partly depend on this.[46] Brown was infuriated when he was excluded from a key trip to Washington to talk about all this. "What did he [Wilson] pledge?" he asked:

> I don't know: that we wouldn't devalue and full support in the Far East. But both those have to go. We've got to turn down their money and pull out the troops. All of them, I don't want them out of Germany. I want them out of east of Suez. This is the decision we have got to make: break the commitment to America.[47]

Even the Chancellor, Jim Callaghan, for all his Atlanticism and previous fondness for the notion of Commonwealth, agreed. Visits to Vietnam convinced him that the US strategy in that country would not succeed, and that Britain's trying to support a policy of the strategic containment of communism in Southeast Asia was basically unnecessary. Accordingly he launched a determined Treasury-led campaign to end the commitment even if it did mean friction with his old colleague, Lee Kuan Yew. These ideas gained traction with the Prime Minister, Harold Wilson, who was acutely aware of the basic point that Britain was spending more on defence as a proportion of its hard-pressed Gross National Product (GNP) than any other industrial competitor bar the United States.[48] Accordingly the decision was taken. East of Suez would have to go. The only question remaining was when, how, and how much.

A Cumulative and Accelerating Decision

After all the public agonizing in London, the leaders of Malaysia, Singapore, Australia, New Zealand and the United States could hardly have been surprised by the announcement that the British were intending to relinquish their role East of Suez. None of them welcomed the decision. In marked contrast to the departure of the French and the Dutch from the scene, the imminent British departure was much lamented. Lee Kuan Yew put it thus in a much quoted passage:

> Britain and the empire constituted the world that I had known all my
> life, a world in which the British were central to our survival; while we
> wanted freedom to decide what we should do with our lives, we also
> wanted and needed our long historical, cultural and economic ties to be
> maintained.[49]

In Kuala Lumpur, the view was much the same, although more diverse.

But what really did raise the ire of leaders in all the partner countries
and the United States were the unnerving speed and the extent of the British
departure. It was a process with insufficient real consultation that bore,
said Dean Rusk, the "acrid aroma of the *fait accompli*."[50] Originally Healey
had had in mind a complete withdrawal by 1975, but to establish an air
and naval base in Australia by then, and merely to halve UK forces and
civilians by 1970–71. The 1966 Defence White Paper specifically stated that
it was "right that Britain should continue to maintain a military presence
in the area", and that the nature of that presence would depend on the
arrangements to be made with our "Commonwealth partners and other
allies in the coming years".[51] Australia, New Zealand and the United States
had got wind of this before the SEATO meeting in Washington and were
extremely critical, and until July 1966 when the Supplementary Defence
White Paper was produced, tried to change Britain's mind. After that, they
all understood the need for reductions but not the prospect of a complete
withdrawal. Lee Kuan Yew was concerned about the economic prospects
of Singapore if the base closed and insufficient security measures had been
taken to ensure future investment in the country.[52] In Kuala Lumpur the
Tunku and Tun Razak had their concerns too.

The 1967 Supplementary Defence White Paper hinted at an acceleration
of the rate of withdrawal, and referred rather obscurely to "the maintenance
of a military capability for use, if required, in the area, even when we no
longer have forces permanently based there".[53] Worse, the Defence White
Paper of January 1968 sped the completion of the process of withdrawal
up from 1975 to 31 March 1971. George Thompson, Secretary of State for
Commonwealth Affairs, came out that month and made the extent of
the cuts clear. "This was a removal of commitments with a vengeance",
remarked General Michael Carver.[54]

The local reaction to this process of acceleration was even more
hostile.[55] Lee Kuan Yew was dismayed by the apparent willingness of a
Labour Government with whose leaders he had got on well "to abdicate
or downgrade their principles". The Malaysians accused Britain of not
honouring the AMDA; it undermined the Tunku's belief in Britain, partly

explaining a turn to France to equip his Air Force and Army, and the "hate Britain" weeks which followed.[56] Australia and New Zealand were very critical too. Australian Prime Minister Robert Menzies had always been prophetic. "He knew where Australia's interests lay; and he did not doubt that they were being sacrificed after Australians had shed blood in two world wars for Britain."[57] The only concession such criticisms wrung from a Britain resolute in its economic weakness, was a nine month delay in the final departure to 31 December 1971. It seemed as bad as bad could be, dishearteningly reminiscent of the final British scuttle from Singapore in 1942.

Negotiating the FPDA

And yet, there remained a little ray of sunshine. While the British were not prepared to take on any significant commitments after the withdrawal, they said they intended to keep to their obligations under the AMDA though without ear-marking forces for it. "It was", remarked General Carver drily, "by no means clear how we could do this."[58] If this was a serious intention then the British would need a re-entry point and a Commonwealth military command organization of some sort, plus of course the re-appearing forces and the willingness to provide them. Instead, however, it was clear that Britain would make no contribution to re-entry facilities in Malaysia or Singapore. There would be no "special capability" for the Far East, but that if the government wished there would be a "general capability" retained in Europe, which would be available for use elsewhere "if in our judgment it is right to do so".[59] The concept and even the language of these discussions were disturbingly reminiscent of British policy towards the relief of Singapore before and into the Second World War, hardly an encouraging precedent. Nor was Britain's marked reluctance to get embroiled in the feud between Malaysia and the Philippines over Sabah in 1968–69 encouraging.[60]

In fact some of the groundwork for a continuing military relationship had already been done. Shortly after George Thompson's appearance in the area, in January 1968 General Carver had set up first an "air defence advisory working group team" and later its army and naval equivalents of the five nations to discuss the mechanics of an orderly withdrawal and in a pragmatic way to make the best of things so that Britain's retreat would seem dignified and orderly. Only Malaysia and New Zealand were enthusiastic about this approach. The Australian and British governments were extremely wary of being trapped into commitments they could not in conscience support. Two months later in March 1968, Malaysia suggested Five Power talks in Kuala Lumpur and personnel from the three working parties met to co-ordinate ideas before the meeting, which was held in June 1968.

At this meeting, the main topic of discussion was the setting up of an integrated air defence system at Butterworth. The notorious Defence White Paper of 1968 claimed that "firm foundations for new defence arrangements were laid by the Five Power Conference held in Kuala Lumpur on 10 and 11 June 1968...."[61] The Labour Government said they wanted to keep on training in the area, and promised that Britain would participate in an exercise involving major reinforcement from Britain in 1970. The idea behind this was to explore just how quickly British reinforcements could be got out to Malaysia should the need arise, and was reported by the new Prime Minister, Edward Heath, later in March 1971, as successful although it did emphasis the importance of having sufficient deterrent forces already in theatre.[62] So, in all these ways, the seed had been sown for the retention of some kind of British military presence in the theatre provided some means could be found to make all this possible. The prospects for this briefly seemed further enhanced by the victory of the new Conservative Government under Mr Heath in June 1970, for the Conservatives had been publicly very critical of the withdrawal from East of Suez, when in opposition.

Lord Carrington, the new Secretary for Defence, came out to see if he could discover some formula that would make this residual commitment seem respectable while sufficiently effective. The three functional groups set up to coordinate the withdrawal by General Carver and carried on by his relief Admiral Sir Peter Hill Norton from March 1969 had already done much of the groundwork for this. But this was to be no last-minute reprieve for a major British presence, as anyone closely monitoring what the Conservatives had actually said during their period of opposition should have realized. Instead it was to be something entirely new. In Sydney on 31 July 1970, Carrington laid out the ground rules. There was to be no complete withdrawal but the new commitment was not to be seen as an "attack of imperial nostalgia". Instead Britain would be a partner equal to the other four, and proceeding only with their complete agreement and support. Any undertakings entered into would be of a political and "consultative" nature rather than an automatic military commitment. It would involve naval, air, and land forces but of a notably modest character and equivalent to that of Britain's four partners.[63] Britain, in short, was to be a security facilitator, not a security provider.[64] The British clearly saw the FPDA as a convenient cover for abandoning AMDA, with its commitment to help defend Eastern Malaysia.[65]

In effect this meant four Nimrod aircraft, a flight of Whirlwind helicopters, a battalion in Malaysia plus five destroyers/frigates and an *Oberon* class submarine generally deployed East of Suez.[66] When asked in Parliament what was the threat against which the new arrangements should be measured, Mr Heath referred to the "threats to Malaysia from the forces outside in Southern Thailand and north of the Malaysian border".[67] And so the Arrangements were agreed.[68]

Yet almost immediately, there were further major reductions in the continuing force levels originally proposed. The notion that Britain's tri-service commitment would amount to some 4,500 men was gone by 1976 and in numerical terms the slow decline has continued ever since. *HMS Richmond*, the Type 23 frigate expected out in Singapore to mark the 40th anniversary of the FPDA in 2011 will be the first British warship to appear in Southeast Asia waters for two years, such are the distractions of the rest of the Indian Ocean.

The FPDA: A Success Story from the UK's Perspective

A brief look back at Britain's original objectives in Southeast Asia seems to suggest that the modest and almost accidental FPDA has turned out to be a surprisingly successful means of achieving them. Britain has, despite everything, managed to retain a toe-hold in the area. Indeed the extent to which Britain's total withdrawal from East of Suez was a chimera almost from the start was becoming obvious before the 1970s ended, with periodic naval group deployments into the Pacific and from 1979, the institution of the Armilla Patrol. Through the Iraq–Iran tanker war of the 1980s, and the first Gulf War, Britain's defence emphasis has been increasingly on the vast area "East of Suez". With just a brief pull-back into the Balkans in the 1990s, the trend of Britain's defence priorities back to the East has accelerated with the Afghanistan campaign being now officially regarded, for better or worse, as the "main effort". The only difference of course is that the *extent* of the commitment is severely limited by the simple fact that British defence expenditure is much less than half of what it was in 1971.

Leaving such grand strategic considerations aside, what of the more immediate objectives of the FPDA? First, as a means of sustaining the spirit and fellowship of the Commonwealth it has been an arrangement by which Singapore, Malaysia, New Zealand, Australia and Britain have managed to stay together in support of a relationship that none of them want to see drastically changed. It is not the only, or even the most important, means of such Commonwealth cooperation of course, but its relaxed and informal character means that it does not compete with any of the alternatives.

Second, it has proved helpful in sustaining the area's security. It has helped ease the potentially fractious relationship between Malaysia and Singapore. In the early days, especially Singapore's sense of vulnerability to Malaysian pressure, not least on its water supplies, increased its determination to develop the military capabilities to look after itself. General Carver's worry, in turn, was that this pursuit of real military capability, especially in the development of a modern air force might set off an arms race with Malaysia and a general sense in both countries that the real purpose of their armed forces was to be prepared to fight each other.[69] The FPDA deserves some of the credit for helping to produce an atmosphere in which, to quote Razak, "as two separate territories, we talk to each other as equals. Where ever we can agree, we work together. If we cannot agree, well, we wait a while."[70]

Part of the business of sustaining the areas' security has been to help build up the military capacity of Singapore and Malaysia. The three "travelling nations" all have a long and rich store of operational experience, producing personnel stationed in the theatre (and the many augmentees brought in for exercises) with specialized roles such as beach clearance, embarked air traffic controllers, logisticians, naval gunfire support directors, and "handlers" for people from the media, nongovernmental organizations and other government departments. Specialists like this are real force multipliers. Above all perhaps, their near continuous involvement in demanding operations has given the British significant experience in the operations of a joint force headquarters, which can be imparted to its local partners. The steady and developing pattern of FPDA exercises into new areas, such as disaster relief, has also been an invaluable means of helping Singapore and Malaysia build up their military skill base. It is not moreover a one-way street, for the exercises in Southeast Asia hone up British military skills too, providing opportunities to explore such things as the impact of local climatic conditions on British equipment and operational procedures.

Third, the FPDA and the conditional promise of security that it provided helped secure the area against the challenge of external threat, perhaps particularly in and for Singapore. Alec Douglas-Home, the future Conservative Foreign Secretary, summed it up quite well:

> ...Lee wants us to stay there not in any great strength but on a scale which would provide a visible token of commitment and be the core round which a five-power arrangement in which he would have confidence could be built up.[71]

The residual presence of the British in Singapore helping, until 1975, to consolidate the Arrangements, said Lee Kuan Yew "...gave us time to sort out our relations with Indonesia without making precipitate moves we might later regret."[72] This was the start of a general policy in Singapore to bring in outsiders where necessary to massage local power imbalances in the region.[73] Despite early indications that it might, this policy has not after all conflicted with the emphasis on regional cooperation. Thus since 2000, ASEAN members such as Indonesia, Brunei, Thailand, and Vietnam are regularly invited to attend the FPDA exercises as observers.

Fourthly, the threat of communism to the area has almost disappeared and today, as Lee Kuan Yew says, it is "[i]mpossible...to imagine the psychological grip the communists had on the Chinese-speaking in the Singapore and Malaya of the 1950s and 60s." In contributing, if only in a small way to the security of the region, the FPDA contributed to the confidence of both countries. Under President Suharto, communism in Indonesia had in any case evaporated years before the FPDA was set up. The much more dangerous Chinese/Vietnamese example which was the chief justification for the FPDA in the British view, finally proved containable.[74]

Britain's fifth objective was to stay alongside the United States, but there is no doubt that in apparently abandoning its East of Suez role, the British caused disappointment and disapproval in Washington. "I cannot conceal from you", President Johnson told Harold Wilson in January 1968, "my deep dismay upon learning this discouraging news."[75] British influence in Washington inevitably declined.[76] The quiet and unexpected success of the FPDA over time did little to mitigate this, although the United States has shown increasing interest in the concept more recently. But, in fact of course, as already noted, the so-called withdrawal from "East of Suez" was one of those grand historic events that in fact never happened. For better or worse, the British have remained the main ally of the United States in operations East of Suez ever since. It would be hard, though, to argue the case that the British policy that led to the FPDA was a successful example of a clever strategy of *reculer pour mieux sauter*!

One final objective that the British sought in its policy in Southeast Asia was the requirement to achieve its objectives at sustainable cost and at a level of risk that the country would find acceptable. The essentially "consultative" nature of the arrangement, which precluded *automatic* involvement in crises in Southeast Asia, was part of this and so was the modest scale of the commitment. Even so cost has proved an ongoing issue of course, and like the other "travelling nations", the United Kingdom would like to see less cost in terms of process, and meetings and more output. It remains to be seen what impact the 2010 Strategic Defence Review will have on Britain's capacity to supply ships and people to the extent that it would undoubtedly wish to the regular pattern of exercises that have made the FPDA the quiet success that it has so far proved to be.

Notes

[1] Lord Carrington, *Reflect on Things Past: The Memoirs of Lord Carrington* (London: Collins, 1988), p. 158; Harold Macmillan, *Riding the Storm 1956–59* (London: Macmillan, 1971), pp. 396–97; John Campbell, *Edward Heath: A Biography* (London: Jonathan Cape, 1993), p. 227. I am grateful to Malcolm Murfett of the National University of Singapore for the opportunity to read an early version of his paper, "The Times They are A Changing", in *Churchill and the Lion City: Shaping Modern Singapore*, edited by Brian Farrell (Singapore: NUS, 2011).

[2] Denis Healey, *The Time of My Life* (London: Penguin, 1989), p. 277.

[3] James Callaghan, *Time and Change* (London: Collins, 1987), p. 58.

[4] Angus Wilson, *The Strange Ride of Rudyard Kipling* (London: Secker and Warburg, 1977), p. 137.

[5] The most accessible and comprehensive compilation of the essential British documents is to be found in *British Documents on the End of Empire*, Series A, Volume 5, *East of Suez and the Commonwealth*, Part I, *East of Suez*, edited by S.R. Ashton and W.R. Louis (London: TSO for the Institute of Commonwealth Studies, 2004), pp. 1–150, 289–394.

[6] As cited in Archana Sharma, *British Policy towards Malaysia 1957–1967* (London: Sangam Books, 1993), p. 46.

[7] Callaghan, *Time and Change*, op. cit., p. 126.

[8] As cited in Sharma, *British Policy towards Malaysia*, op. cit., p. 16.

9   Speech, 28 February 1967, as quoted in Philip Darby, *British Defence Policy East of Suez* (London: Oxford University Press, 1973), p. 315.

10 Peter Lowe, *Contending with Nationalism and Communism: British Policy towards Southeast Asia* (Basingstoke: Palgrave Macmillan, 2009), p. 45.

11 Memorandum by the Foreign Office, presented to Cabinet Defence and Oversea Policy Committee, 19 November 1964, CAB 148/17, OPD (64) 10, in *British Documents*, edited by Ashton and Louis, p. 295.

12 Report by Official Committee under Sir Burke Trend, 8 November 1965, CAB 130/213, Misc 17/4, in *British Documents*, edited by Ashton and Louis, op. cit., p. 23.

13 Sir Burke Trend Official Committee to the Cabinet Defence and Oversea Policy Committee Report, 10 May 1966, CAB 148/28, OPD (66) 54, in *British Documents*, edited by Ashton and Louis, op. cit., p. 76.

14 Speech to SEATO Council, Manila, 2 July 1970, reproduced in *Current British Foreign Policy 1970*, edited by D.C. Watt and J. Mayall (London: Temple Smith, 1971), p. 369. The same kind of thinking contributed to the founding of ASEAN in 1967 — at least according to Lee Kuan Yew, *The Singapore Story* (Singapore: Marshall Cavendish, 2010), p. 370.

15 Ben Pimlott, *Harold Wilson* (London: Harper Collins, 1992), p. 384.

16 Lowe, *Contending with Nationalism and Communism*, op. cit., p. 251.

17 Defence Review, 8 November 1965, CAB 130/213, Misc 17/4, in *British Documents*, edited by Ashton and Louis, op. cit., p. 28.

18 Chin Kin Wah, *The Defence of Malaysia and Singapore: Transformation of a Security System 1957–1971* (Cambridge: Cambridge University Press, 1983), p. 24.

19 CAB 148/28, OPD (66) 54, in *British Documents*, edited by Ashton and Louis, op. cit., p. 76. For this reason the British doubted the future security of bases in Singapore and Malaysia, and this provided another incentive for leaving.

20 Lowe, *Contending with Nationalism and Communism*, op. cit., pp. 54–55; Chandran Jeshuran, *Malaysia: 50 Years of Diplomacy* (Singapore: Talisman Publishing Pte Ltd, 2008), pp. 32–37; Sharma, *British Policy towards Malaysia*, op. cit., pp. 41, 47. The justification for the British deploying nuclear weapons into Southeast Asia, of course, was the supposed threat posed by Communist China.

21 Darby, *British Defence Policy East of Suez*, op. cit., p. 291.

22 Kenneth O. Morgan, *Callaghan: A Life* (Oxford: Oxford University Press, 1997), pp. 144–45; Harold Wilson, *The Labour Government 1964–1970: A Personal Record* (London: Weidenfeld and Nicolson, 1971), pp. 130–31.

23 Carrington, *Reflect on Things Past*, op. cit., p. 238.

24 Campbell, *Edward Heath*, op. cit., p. 337.

25 Carrington, *Reflect on Things Past*, op. cit., pp. 284–85; Wilson, *The Labour Government*, op. cit., p. 116.

26 Ibid.

27 Ibid., p. 145.
28 Campbell, *Edward Heath*, op. cit., pp. 289, 310.
29 Denis Healey, "British Defence Policy", lecture at the Royal United Services Institute, 22 October 1969, *RUSI Journal*, p. 16.
30 Darby introduces this point, *British Defence Policy East of Suez*, op. cit., pp. 122–24.
31 Lowe, *Contending with Nationalism and Communism*, op. cit., p. 46.
32 CAB 148/28 OPD (66) 54, in *British Documents*, edited by Ashton and Louis, op. cit., p. 78.
33 Defence and Overseas Policy Committee, Report of September 1964, as cited in David Easter, *Britain and the Confrontation with Indonesia 1960–66* (London: I.B. Tauris, 2004), pp. 110–12; in *British Documents*, edited by Ashton and Louis, op. cit., p. 299.
34 Carrington, *Reflect on Things Past*, op. cit., p. 158.
35 Defence review: forces structure and overseas commitments, minutes of Cabinet Defence and Overseas Policy Committee, 1 February 1966, CAB 148/25, OPD 9 (66) 1, in *British Documents*, edited by Ashton and Louis, op. cit., p. 68.
36 Ian Speller, "The Royal Navy, Expeditionary Operations and the End of Empire, 1956–75", in *British Naval Strategy East of Suez, 1900–2000*, edited by Greg Kennedy (London: Frank Cass, 2005), pp. 181–82; Carrington, *Reflect on Things Past*, op. cit., p. 176.
37 Lee, *The Singapore Story*, op. cit., pp. 466–69.
38 Ibid., p. 573. This was before the election which Wilson felt confident he would win. Pimlott, *Harold Wilson*, op. cit., p. 369; Chris Tuck, "The Royal Navy and Confrontation 1963–66", in *British Naval Strategy*, edited by Kennedy.
39 As cited in Tuck, "The Royal Navy and Confrontation", p. 203; DEFE/5/155, COS 242/64, Directive to the Commander-in-Chief Far East in the event of Indonesia attempting to interfere with Commonwealth Shipping, 20 August 1964.
40 Lee, *The Singapore Story*, op. cit., p. 523.
41 Easter, *Britain and the Confrontation with Indonesia*, op. cit., pp. 174–92. They were operationally risky too; see Darby, *British Defence Policy East of Suez*, op. cit., p. 271.
42 Tuck, "The Royal Navy and Confrontation", op. cit., p. 214.
43 Michael Carver, *Out of Step: The Memoirs of Field Marshal Lord Carver*, (London: Hutchinson, 1989) p. 2; Wilson, *The Labour Government*, op. cit., p. 233.
44 Morgan, *Callaghan*, op. cit., pp. 203, 210–12; Campbell, *Edward Heath*, op. cit., p. 225; Pimlott, *Harold Wilson*, op. cit., pp. 405, 433.
45 Callaghan, *Time and Change*, op. cit., pp. 159, 167.
46 The idea of a large US loan appeared in February 1967 — in return for Britain keeping its East of Suez role. See for instance, Minute by A.M. Palliser of

28 July 1965, FO 371/180543, no. 188, in *British Documents*, edited by Ashton and Louis, op. cit., p. 337. This was unacceptable to Callaghan even though he was an avowed Atlanticist. See also, Callaghan, *Time and Change*, op. cit., pp. 118, 211; Morgan, *Callaghan*, op. cit., p. 225.

47 Sharma, *British Policy towards Malaysia*, op. cit., p. 433.

48 Morgan, *Callaghan*, op. cit., p. 18.

49 Lee, *The Singapore Story*, op. cit., p. 455.

50 Telegram from George Brown, 12 January 1968, in *British Documents*, edited by Ashton and Louis, op. cit., p. 132.

51 London: Defence White Paper, 1966, p. 8.

52 Lee Kuan Yew, *From Third World to First* (Singapore: Marshall Cavendish, 2000), p. 52; Carver, *Out of Step*, op. cit., pp. 357–58, 372.

53 1967 Cmnd 3357, *Supplementary Statement on Defence Policy* (London: HMSO, July 1967), pp. 4, 6.

54 Carver, *Out of Step*, op. cit., p. 368.

55 See *British Documents*, edited by Ashton and Louis, op. cit., pp. 373–88.

56 Carver, *Out of Step*, op. cit., p. 387.

57 Lee, *The Singapore Story*, op. cit., p. 457.

58 Carver, *Out of Step*, op. cit., p. 369.

59 Ibid., p. 371.

60 Ibid., pp. 376, 382–87.

61 1968 Cmnd 3540, *Statement on The Defence Estimates 1968* (London: HMSO, Feb 1968), p. 4.

62 Edward Heath, "Speech in House of Commons, 2 March 1971", reproduced in *Current British Foreign Policy*, edited by Watt and Mayall, op. cit., p. 78.

63 Lord Carrington, "Speech at the National Press Club, Sydney, 31 July 1970", reproduced in *Current British Foreign Policy*, edited by Watt and Mayall, op. cit., pp. 438–40.

64 Christopher Hill and Christopher Lord, "The Foreign Policy of the Heath Government", in *The Heath Government*, edited by Stuart Ball and Anthony Seldon (London: Longman, 1996), pp. 290–91.

65 *British Documents on the End of Empire*, edited by Ashton and Louis, op. cit., p. 80.

66 Ibid., p. 65.

67 Heath, "Speech in House of Commons", p. 78; Carrington, *Reflect on Things Past*, op. cit., pp. 219–20.

68 The full text of Britain's arrangements with Malaysia and Singapore of 1 December 1971 can be found in *Current British Foreign Policy*, edited by Watt and Mayall, op. cit., pp. 1119–37.

69 Carver, *Out of Step*, op. cit., pp. 375–77.

70 Lee, *From Third World to First*, op. cit., p. 63.

71 John K. Hickman, British High Commission to FCO, 11 March 1970, DEFE 68/2, as cited in Murfett, "The Times They are A Changing", op. cit.

72 Lee, *From Third World to First*, op. cit., p. 421.

73 Lily Zubaidah Rahim, *Singapore in the Malay World: Building and Breaching Regional Bridges* (London: Routledge, 2010), pp. 86–91.

74 Lee, *From Third World to First*, op. cit., p. 133; Dennis Bloodworth, *The Tiger and the Trojan Horse* (Singapore: Marshall Cavendish, 2011), pp. 389–414.

75 President Johnson to Harold Wilson, 11 January 1968, Prem 13/1999, no. 8a, in *British Documents*, edited by Ashton and Louis, op. cit., pp. 127–28.

76 Geoffrey Williams and Bruce Reed, *Denis Healey and the Policies of Power* (London: Sidgwick and Jackson, 1971), p. 242.

2

On the Establishment of the Five Power Defence Arrangements (FPDA)

Ang Cheng Guan

On the 40th anniversary of the Five Power Defence Arrangements (FPDA), it is opportune to re-visit the circumstances under which the agreement came into effect on 1 November 1971. Even though London had decided to withdraw from East of Suez as announced in the July 1967 Defence White Paper, it envisaged "continued cooperation with our Commonwealth partners"[1] in the area of security and defence. On 16 January 1968 London informed the Malaysian Government that they "wished to reach a new understanding with them about the Anglo-Malaysian Defence Agreement (AMDA) to make it fit the changed conditions".[2] The withdrawal plan was re-affirmed in the February 1970 Defence White Paper. Soon after in April, the defence secretary, Denis Healey disclosed that the government had proposed a new five power framework to replace AMDA and that he hoped that formal talks could start soon.[3] In June 1970, the Labour Government was unexpectedly defeated by the Conservative Party led by Edward Heath in the June 1970 election and Healey was replaced by Lord (Peter) Carrington as the new defence secretary.

This paper focuses on the fifteen months between July–August 1970 and the establishment of the FPDA on 1 November 1971 for two reasons. First, this period was particularly critical in the formation of the FPDA. One would have thought that it was quite easy to transit from the AMDA, which had been in existence since 1957, to the FPDA but in fact this was not the case. In reality, it was a period of rather excoriating negotiations. A second reason for focusing on these fifteen months is because it (particularly the Malaysia and Singapore dimension) has never been written about in any detail.

July–August 1970 to the End of 1970

It is against the above background that about a month after assuming his post, the new Defence Secretary Lord Carrington visited Canberra, Wellington, Kuala Lumpur and Singapore from 23 July–3 August. The purpose of the visit was for "a preliminary exchange of views with the Governments concerned about our (British) contribution to future Commonwealth defence arrangements in Southeast Asia". According to Lord Carrington in his report to the Prime Minister, the consultations were "very successful". Although Australia and Malaysia would have liked AMDA to continue, all four countries recognized the reality of the situation and accepted that it should be replaced by "a consultative commitment informally expressed and undertaken equally by all five governments".[4]

Conversations between the British High Commissioner to Malaysia, Sir M. Walker, with Prime Minister Tun Abdul Razak and other senior Malaysian officials soon after Lord Carrington's visit, as well as Australian sources, reveal the following about Malaysia's thinking.[5] From Razak, he learnt that while Malaysia would like AMDA to remain, the proposed "looser" agreement was acceptable. According to Razak, "taking into account Malaysia's concern about the Indonesian attitude towards defence treaties … the less formally this agreement was recorded the better".[6] Razak also reiterated to Walker that he wished Australia to fill the role of Air Defence Commander by combining the position with that of Air Officer Commanding (AOC) in Butterworth (Singapore also concurred on this).[7] With regards to the Jungle Warfare Centre, the British found that the Malaysians wanted the Centre to be seen as a "Malaysian establishment". The Australians were apparently aware that the Malaysian Army and Ministry of Defence were looking to actual Malaysian control of the Centre and believed that they would soon be making a formal approach to all concerned. According to the US Ambassador to Malaysia, Jack Lydman, the Secretary-General at the Malaysian Ministry of Defence, Samad Noor, and several senior Malaysian army officers had tentatively raised the possibility of the United States sending some Special Forces instructors to the Centre. The US Defence Attache was looking into this issue but Ambassador Lydman expected resistance in Washington. The Deputy-Secretary at the Malaysian Ministry of Foreign Affairs, Zainal Abidin Sulong, told the British that although "a group" in the Malaysian government had hoped for a larger British presence, which would have permitted the Malaysians to increase their defence expenditure more gradually, the Malaysian services were "pleased with the outcome" and Kuala Lumpur was "not concerned that no British forces were to be based in Malaysia".[8] Indeed, Australian officials based in Kuala Lumpur already noted in late-July 1970 that there was "a strong strain of disillusionment with the British" and they anticipated that "if the political commitment were unsatisfactory", the Malaysians would rather not have British forces based in Malaysia.[9] Another reason why the Malaysians were hesitant to host British troops was because of the "distrust of Singapore and the feeling that a British presence on Malaysian soil could lead to a Singapore presence also under the Five Power umbrella". There was apparently a "strong dislike in [the Ministry of Defence] MINDEF and Malaysian military circles of opening the door to this". Among the reasons which Samad Noor gave the British High Commission for not having British troops in Malaysia was the "dislike of having Singapore troops in Malaysia".[10] The anti-Singapore attitude was also one reason for Kuala Lumpur's insistence of taking over control of the Jungle Warfare Centre.[11] As the out-going British High Commissioner to Malaysia, Sir Michael Walker noted, the Malaysians were "profoundly distrustful of Singapore".[12] The Australians believed that there was a "differing balance of views" within the Malaysian Government with MINDEF being more "nationalistic", the Ministry of Foreign Affairs (MFA) more "accommodating" and Razak "somewhere between the two".[13]

Malaysia's thinking towards the end of 1970 can be gleaned from two sets of conversations, the first of which was between Zainal Abidin Sulong and officials from the Australian High Commission on 24 November. According to Zainal, with the end of AMDA and the diminished roles of both the United Kingdom and the United States in the region, it was "important politically" for Malaysia to come up with some "alternative".

They were: (a) the doctrine of greater "self-reliance" in defence; (b) the need to develop regional cooperation in defence as in other fields; and (c) the "new look" as regards non-alignment and Malaysia's desire to increase the range of its international friendships, including China.[14]

The second was a "no-holds-barred" conversation between Zain Asraai and the Australian Deputy High Commissioner to Malaysia, A.D. Campbell, in December which covered three major topics: (a) the doctrine of "looseness" for post-AMDA arrangements; (b) Malaysia–Singapore relations; and (c) how to reconcile the policy of neutralism with the FPDA. The Malaysian concern was the connection/overlap between the Air Defence Council (as proposed by the Australians) and the consultative council/body of the FPDA (as proposed by the British). According to Zain, "air defence was the one, and really the only, area where Malaysia's defence forces needed supplementing by visiting forces; hence there was no Malaysian wish for looseness in these arrangements...."[15] The discussion on Malaysia–Singapore relations centred on the Jungle Warfare Centre. The British had apparently submitted to the Malaysians an estimate of the personnel and unit requirements for jungle training of the UK, Australian, New Zealand and Singapore forces despite Tun Razak's insistence that bids must be put in bilaterally for Malaysian consideration. The Malaysians would not move from this position. Given Kuala Lumpur's opposition to Singaporean forces training in Malaysia, this would have implications for Singapore. Zain said that Singapore–Malaysian relations were "complex, hard to follow, and unpredictable". Jungle training was only one of a number of issues between both countries and Johor politics played a part in several of them. The solution, according to Zain, would not be worked out in isolation from other problems between the two countries. As this was a bilateral problem, it would not be discussed at the January 1971 meeting. As for the policy of neutralism and the FPDA, Zain simply insisted that there was no conflict between the two. The public position taken by Malaysian ministers was that "the policy objective of neutralism and the Five Power arrangements were entirely consistent". The government "did not intend arguing, or seeking to justify it, in public". In any case, Malaysia would be "very very cautious" in pursuing its neutralization policy. At some point in the future, Zain postulated, when there was genuine neutralization in the region, contradiction might arise but by then the five power arrangements might also no longer be relevant.[16]

As regards the position of Singapore, Prime Minister Lee Kuan Yew too was happy with the Conservative Party's victory. But whereas the Malaysian attitude was to stress that the political commitment of Britain would influence their decision whether or not to have British forces in Malaysia, Singapore's approach was not to rely too heavily on the British presence "but yet to make it easy to maintain" British forces in Singapore.[17] In actual fact, Lee accepted an ANZUK brigade (a tripartite force comprising Australia, New Zealand and the United Kingdom) in Singapore with some reluctance, preferring "sophisticated naval and air units than in ground forces".[18] In the end, he reasoned that a small British force based in Singapore would provide "added security for another 3 ½ to 4 ½ years", allow the government to "readjust our plans and have thorough training for our air and naval forces, and go on to more sophisticated weapons".[19] (That the FPDA could provide a breathing space for Singapore and as well to become more self-reliant was a view shared by Malaysian Deputy Premier Tun Dr Ismail).[20]

The record of a discussion between Lord Carrington and Prime Minister Lee on 5 October 1970 at Whitehall provides a glimpse of the Singaporean leader's thinking during this time. Apparently, it was Lee who had advised Carrington to probe the Malaysians on the questioning of stationing some British troops in Malaysia. Carrington informed Lee that he had probed the Malaysians "to the point of rudeness" but had received no clearer response than that they were short of accommodation for their own army and would find it hard to find space for British forces, unless London really wanted it. Lee said that he was quite content to let that matter lie. Lee told Carrington that he did not fully understand Razak's "public insistence upon an independent defence and foreign policy" though he suspected that Razak "was putting probably rationalizing an unsatisfactory situation and putting on a show".

The report of a meeting between Singapore Defence Minister Dr Goh Keng Swee and the New Zealand High Commissioner on 10 November 1970 sheds considerable light on Goh's view about the FPDA and Singapore–Malaysia relations during this period.[21] According to the report, Goh "showed every sign of being absolutely worried about the deterioration of relations between Singapore and Malaysia". He hoped that the High Commissioner would report back the conversation to the New Zealand Government and "if things got any worse", Singapore might consider asking Wellington to persuade Kuala Lumpur "to take a more reasonable attitude". Goh highlighted a number of issues: Malaysia was accusing Singapore of "stealing" good men from the Malaysian Armed Forces for the Singapore Armed Forces (SAF). Goh conceded it had accepted some who claimed Singapore citizenship and who had opted out of the Malaysian Armed Services. He was tightening up procedures and was trying to work out some understanding with Kuala Lumpur but "they will not listen"; Malaysia refused to allow a Singapore naval training ship to call at Port Swettenham (now Port Klang) and would not give any reason for it; Malaysia wanted to restrict Singaporean use of the Jungle Warfare Centre; Malaysia was determined not to let Singapore use China Rock for bombing practice; there were problems related to the splitting up of the Malaysia–Singapore Airline (MSA). The "most serious issue" was that of water supplies. Singapore was anxious to proceed with its plans for expanding its reservoirs but its approach for a loan from the Asia Development Bank (ADB) was "being jeopardized by Malaysian refusal to give its consent".[22] There was, according to Goh, a "whole range of minor matters over which the Malaysians were being more than usually sticky".

With regards to the FPDA, Goh was of the view that the Arrangements were "essential particularly as a means of bringing Singapore and Malaysia together". The Malaysians, according to Goh, needed the FPDA too. Kuala Lumpur needed British, Australian and New Zealand forces in the area as an ultimate assurance that they could call for help "if things go sour". All these cries for closer relation with China and the emphasis on neutrality (Zone of Peace, Freedom and Neutrality, ZOPFAN) were "window dressing". "The Malaysians knew", Goh said, "if they could not rely on Britain, Australia, and New Zealand, they would have to turn to the Indonesians and Razak knew the Indonesians would gobble him up."[23]

Given the poor state of Singapore–Malaysia relations, Lee Kuan Yew was concerned about training facilities for the SAF. During a meeting with the British High Commissioner to Singapore, Sam Falle, on 9 December 1970, he informed Falle that he was already in touch with Canberra regarding allowing Singaporean troops to exercise on Australian soil. This, according to Lee, was not solely related to the jungle warfare training. Lee also enquired about the possibility of using Brunei (in lieu of China Rock) for air defence training. Lee further requested that Britain station a company of troops in Johor "leaving their families in Singapore, so that they would not be in danger from race riots". His ostensible reason was that "the

Malaysians were so insecure in themselves that they would welcome even a very small British presence". Lee believed that Kuala Lumpur's insecurity was driving the Malaysians closer to Indonesia.[24] The Australians noted that one of the chief attractions of having British forces actually stationed in Malaysia was its "effect on confidence", which Second Deputy Prime Minister Tun Dr Ismail understood but others did not.[25]

According to a Foreign and Commonwealth Office memorandum of 14 December 1970, Dr Goh had approached the British about the possibility of Australia providing training space for Singapore's tank and armoured personnel carriers. What Goh had in mind was the possibility of stationing a number of tanks and vehicles in Australia and rotate a company of trainees each time. According to the memorandum, the approach arose from the problems created for Singapore by "the Malaysian reluctance to provide access by Singapore to the Commonwealth Jungle Warfare Centre (CJWC) and to training areas in Malaysia".[26]

Goh also met Falle on 17 December 1970 regarding Singapore air defence training in Brunei. According to Goh, "this was in addition to facilities they still hope to obtain at China Rock, not merely instead of China Rock if the Malaysians should not make this available". Apparently, Goh had told the Australians that Singapore also hoped to conduct jungle warfare training in Brunei although neither Lee nor Goh mentioned this in their meetings with Falle.[27]

7–8 January 1971: Five Power Officials Talks on Defence in Singapore

Officials representing the Five Powers met in Singapore in January 1971 to prepare for the London meeting in April. The Five Power Official Talks, in the words of the leader of the British delegation, Patrick Nairne, "went rather better than we had expected". There were as expected some "undercurrents", for example, both Secretary-General, Malaysian Ministry of Foreign Affairs and Leader of the Malaysian delegation Tan Sri Zaiton and Secretary-General, Malaysian Ministry of Defence, Samad Noor, told the Australians that they could accept the word "indivisibility" of Malaysia and Singapore's defence in Paragraph 3 but did not wish to have any reference to the need for "cooperation" between the two countries in the text. Zaiton explained that they did not want to expose themselves to domestic criticism about relations with Singapore.[28] On the whole, however, the British reported that "at no time was anything said indicating distrust or discrimination towards Singapore, though this still lies below the surface".[29] By the time of the Singapore meeting, it was already clear that Malaysia would control the Jungle Warfare Centre. None of the other governments supported the British proposal of multilateral ownership.[30] Soon after the Singapore meeting, an Anglo-Malaysia Working Group was formed to draw up a plan for the conversion of the Centre into a Malaysian Army Training Centre by January 1972.

The meeting in London took place on 15–16 April 1971. A ministerial communiqué was issued on 16 April which essentially reflected the earlier agreements in Singapore.[31] The remaining unfinished business was the negotiations with Malaysia and Singapore on the Annexes (issues pertaining to the status of forces, legal matters, questions of tenure, real estate etc.). The Five Power Ministers had directed that the negotiations should be completed by mid-June, but given the pace of the negotiations it was hoped that it could be completed in time before the termination of AMDA on 1 November 1971.[32] The British were particularly concerned about the "slow progress". Much time was spent discussing the Jungle Warfare Centre with the British and "presentational issues", which made the negotiating process "cumbersome".

In the case of Singapore, negotiations, which had been going "reasonably well", had stalled since mid-May. The issue was over rent and training facilities. Singapore drove a hard bargain. Initially, Singapore wanted Britain, Australia and New Zealand to pay rent but subsequently waived it for the British only. As Lord Carrington said, given the amount of real estate and assets that the British were giving to Singapore for free, "it would be intolerable to pay rent to Singapore and such a course could not be defended in Parliament".[33] Canberra and Wellington felt very strongly that all ANZUK forces should be treated equally, a view that London shared.[34] And it is this subject we now turn to.

I shall highlight just one conversation to illustrate the real issue. This is a record of a meeting between Goh Keng Swee and the Australian High Commissioner to Singapore, Nicholas Parkinson, on 8 June 1971. Goh had wanted to meet Parkinson to check whether the Australian side had received Singapore's training requests. Goh wanted Parkinson to understand "what the game was all about" with regard to rent and training. In Goh's words, the "whole Five Power business was a toothless paper tiger". There were only two possible threats to Singapore and they were

Indonesia and Malaysia, and the FPDA would be of no use in addressing either. Thus if Canberra would not accede to Singapore's request for training facilities, "you can go home". Singapore would be informing him of the rent figures soon and he hoped that the Australians would find the rent demand "exorbitant" and realize that the only option was to accede to Singapore's training requests or "go home". If Australia provided the training facilities, Singapore would waive "the rent altogether". Singapore would also pay for all training requirements in Australia. Most important to Singapore were air and armour training. When Parkinson reiterated the difficulties Australia faced in acceding to Singapore's requests, Goh retorted that what he needed was "constructive help" and not the constant harping of the difficulties. There was also no use asking Singapore to seek facilities from Malaysia as "Singapore knew perfectly well that Malaysia would not allow Singapore tank or aircraft to train in Malaysia". Parkinson asked Goh whether he should tell Canberra that the Singapore government would opt out of the FPDA unless Australia acceded to Singapore's request. Goh's reply was "Yes....Tell them that bluntly". Goh had in fact moved his position from "provide us with training or pay rent" (which was what he told Australian Defence Minister John Gorton when they met in London in April 1971) to the extreme position of "provide us with training or go home". Parkinson, in his report, said he was sure there was some "bluff and overstatement" in what Goh said but it was difficult to judge how much.[35] The follow-up letter from Goh was more moderate in tone, although the intention remained unchanged. In his letter of 10 June, Goh explained Singapore's request: "Basically, the proposal is to station a small amount of military hardware in training areas in Australia, together with maintenance crews, and to rotate operational personnel and train them in the use of these weapons and equipment".[36]

The British side was deeply concerned with the situation and in their discussions with the Australians, they expressed hope that Canberra could accede to as much, if not all, of Singapore's training requests. London would also do what it could to help Singapore with its training needs. In the British assessment, the Indonesians and the Malaysians would not strongly oppose it.[37] The chief Malaysian objection, according to the Australians, was tank training.[38]

Eventually, on 3 July, Australian Prime Minister William McMahon announced that the Australian Government had agreed to a request by Singapore for their troops to train in Australia. McMahon further added that Kuala Lumpur had not made a similar request and if there was any, it would be considered under the terms of the FPDA. Foreign Minister Leslie Bury explained at a press conference in Kuala Lumpur in July 1971 that the reason for Singapore's request was because there was little training space in Singapore as the island was too tightly-knit and heavily populated. He further revealed that Malaysia was "not altogether delighted but was reasonably reconciled" to Singapore troops training in Australia.[39] The settlement on the training issue paved the way for the resolution of the rent negotiation,[40] which made it possible to complete the negotiations for the FPDA to come into force on 1 November 1971.

Notes

[1]   Derek McDougall, "Australia and the British Military Withdrawal from East of Suez", *Australian Journal of International Affairs* 51, no. 2 (1997): 186.

[2]   Anglo-Malaysian Defence Agreement (AMDA), British proposal for replacement by Five Power Declaration (For Cabinet) (Secret), A/5869, Item 316.

[3]   Ibid., p. 171.

[4]   Draft DPOC Paper on UK Military Presence in Southeast Asia, 29 September 1970 (Secret), FCO 24/653, National Archives of Singapore, Microfilm Number NAB 1635.

[5]   From Kuala Lumpur to Department of External Affairs, Canberra, 18 August 1970 (Secret), A4359, Item 221/4/31/4 PART 1; From Kuala Lumpur to Department of External Affairs, Canberra, Post-AMDA Arrangements, 20 August 1970 (Secret), A4359, Item 221/4/31/4 PART 1.

[6]   See also, From Kuala Lumpur to Department of External Affairs, Canberra, Renewal of British Presence, 27 July 1970 (Secret), A4359, Item 221/4/31/4 PART 1 for another observation of Indonesia as a factor in Malaysia's unwillingness to seek a formal treaty.

[7]   See Paragraph 4 of Summary Record of the Five Power Official Talks on Defence, Singapore, 7–8 January 1971, Annex A: Speech by Mr Pang Tee Pow (Secret), FCO 24/975, National Archives of Singapore, Microfilm Number NAB 1402.

[8]   From Kuala Lumpur to Department of External Affairs, Canberra, 18 August 1970 (Secret), A4359, Item 221/4/31/4 PART 1; From Kuala Lumpur to Department of External Affairs, Canberra, Post-AMDA Arrangements, 20 August 1970 (Secret), A4359, Item 221/4/31/4 PART 1.

[9]   From Kuala Lumpur to Department of External Affairs, Canberra, Renewal of British Presence, 27 July 1970 (Secret), A4359, Item 221/4/31/4 PART 1.

[10] Ibid.

[11] Department of External Affairs, Record of Conversation: Five Power Arrangements, 15 October 1970 (Confidential), A4359, Item 221/4/31/4 PART 1.

12 Foreign and Commonwealth Office, Malaysia: Annual Review for 1970, Diplomatic Report No. 51/71 (Confidential), FCO 24/1151, National Archives of Singapore, Microfilm Number NAB 1479.

13 From Kuala Lumpur to Department of External Affairs, Canberra, Renewal of British Presence, 27 July 1970 (Secret), A4359, Item 221/4/31/4 PART 1.

14 From Kuala Lumpur to Department of External Affairs, Canberra, 24 November 1970 (Confidential), A4359, Item 221/4/31/4 PART 2.

15 The headquarters of the Integrated Air Defence System (IADS) was formed in Butterworth on 11 February 1971 with an Australian commander (Air Vice-Marshal R.T. Susans) and became operational on 1 September 1971.

16 From Kuala Lumpur to Department of External Affairs, Canberra, Record of Conversation: Some Aspects of the Malaysian Approach to Five Power Arrangements, 17 December 1970 (Confidential), A4359, Item 221/4/31/4 PART 2.

17 From Kuala Lumpur to Department of External Affairs, Canberra, Renewal of British Presence, 27 July 1970 (Secret), A4359, Item 221/4/31/4 PART 1.

18 Singapore: Annual Review for 1970 and Some Personal First Impressions, 1 January 1977 (Confidential), FCO 24/1193, National Archives of Singapore, Microfilm Number NAB 1909.

19 From Singapore to Department of External Affairs, Canberra, Savingram 2/70, 24 July 1970, A1838, 696/1/9/PART 12 as cited in Andrea Benvenuti and Moreen Dee, "The Five Power Defence Arrangements and the Reappraisal of the British and Australian Policy Interests in Southeast Asia, 1970–1975", *Journal of Southeast Asian Studies* 41, no. 1 (2010): 108.

20 Kuala Lumpur to Department of External Affairs, Canberra, Cablegram 2660, 1 July 1970, A1838, 696/1/9/PART 12 as cited in Benvenuti and Dee, "The Five Power Defence Arrangements", p. 109.

21 From Singapore to Wellington, 10 November 1970 (Confidential), FCO 24/655, National Archives of Singapore, Microfilm Number NAB 1636.

22 For Goh's recounting of the water supplies issue to New Zealand Deputy High Commissioner John Hickman of which a copy of the report of meeting was sent to the FCO, see From Singapore to Foreign and Commonwealth Office, Telegram Number 893, 20 November 1970 (Confidential), FCO 24/894, National Archives of Singapore, Microfilm Number NAB 1260.

23 From Singapore to Wellington, 10 November 1970 (Confidential), FCO 24/655, National Archives of Singapore, Microfilm Number NAB 1636.

24 From Singapore to Foreign and Commonwealth Office, Telegram Number 968, 9 December 1970 (Confidential), FCO 24/656, National Archives of Singapore, Microfilm Number NAB 1260.

25 From Kuala Lumpur to Department of External Affairs, Canberra, Renewal of British Presence, 27 July 1970 (Secret), A4359, Item 221/4/31/4 PART 1.

26 Training by Singapore Armed Forces in Australia, 14 December 1970

(Confidential), FCO 24/656, National Archives of Singapore, Microfilm Number NAB 1260.

27 From Singapore to Foreign and Commonwealth Office, 17 December 1970 (Confidential), FCO 24/657, National Archives of Singapore, Microfilm Number NAB 1260.

28 From Singapore to Department of External Affairs, Canberra, 4 January 1971 (Secret), A4359, Item 221/4/31/4 PART 2.

29 From Singapore to Foreign and Commonwealth Office, Five Power Talks, 9 January 1971 (Confidential), FCP, 24/975, National Archives of Singapore, Microfilm Number NAB 1402.

30 From Singapore to Department of External Affairs, Canberra, 4 January 1971 (Secret), A4359, Item 221/4/31/4 PART 2.

31 For the full text, see From London to Department of External Affairs, Canberra, 16 April 1971, A4359, Item 221/4/31/4 PART 2.

32 Five Power Defence Arrangements: Notes and Annexes, 28 June 1971 (Confidential), FCO 24/1012, National Archives of Singapore, Microfilm Number NAB 1478.

33 Meeting between the Defence Secretary and the New Zealand High Commissioner, 31 March 1971 (Confidential), FCO 24/980, National Archives of Singapore, Microfilm Number NAB 1402; D.M. McBain, "Interview with J.K. Hickman, CMG", 18 December 1995, <http://www.chu.cam.ac.uk/archives/collections/BDOHP/Hickman.pdf>

34 Five Power Defence Arrangements (for inclusion in the PUS's Monthly Newsletter), FCO 24/981, National Archives of Singapore, Microfilm Number NAB 1402.

35 From Singapore to Department of External Affairs, Canberra, 8 June 1971 (Secret), A4359, Item 221/4/31/4 PART 3. Goh subsequently wrote to Parkinson on 10 June 1971.

36 The letter was written in less stark terms compared to the 8 June conversation but the thrust is essentially the same. See From Singapore to Department of External Affairs, Canberra, 10 June 1971 (Secret), A4359, Item 221/4/31/4 PART 3.

37 From London to Department of External Affairs, Canberra, Five Power — Singapore Training and Real Estate, 12 June 1971 (Secret), A4359, Item 221/4/31/4 PART 3.

38 Australian Embassy, Jakarta, Inwards Cablegram from Kuala Lumpur, Singapore Rent and Training, 19 June 1971 (Secret), A4359, Item 221/4/31/4 PART 3.

39 Australian Embassy, Jakarta, Inwards Cablegram from Kuala Lumpur, "Straits Times" Report of 10 July, 10 July 1971, A4359, Item 221/4/31/4 PART 3.

40 Five Power Defence Arrangements Come into Effect (Statement by Minister of Defence, the Hon. David Fairbairn, DFC, MP), 1 November 1971 (For Press), A4359, Item 221/4/31/4 PART 3.

3

Malaysian Foreign Policy and the Five Power Defence Arrangements[1]

Johan Saravanamuttu

The paper examines the role of the Five Power Defence Arrangements (FPDA) in regional security from the perspective of Malaysia. It begins with a framing of Malaysia's defence posture and needs in terms of a transition from conventional defence in the 1950s and 1960s to a security-oriented discourse since the mid-1970s. That transition took place when the Anglo-Malayan Defence Agreement (AMDA) of 1957 was replaced by the FPDA in 1971. Malaysia's non-participation in the South-East Asia Treaty Organization (SEATO) and its insistence that the nuclear weapons option be excluded from AMDA had provided an important context for Malaysia's overall stance on defence and security even during the early years of independence. By the mid-1970s, Malaysia's foreign policy was cast in terms of neutralism and nonalignment. It had found cause in the promotion of a Zone of Peace, Freedom and Neutrality (ZOPFAN) in Southeast Asia and saw an active participation in the Southeast Asia Nuclear Weapon-Free Zone (SEANWFZ). Some may argue that Malaysia's participation in the FPDA compromised such a foreign policy. However, seen from the perspective of regional security, the FPDA was an important construct and confidence building measure (CBM) for the continued involvement of Commonwealth forces in Malaysia's defence and role in regional security. Moreover, the FPDA was especially crucial as a CBM for boosting and maintaining security cooperation between Malaysia and Singapore. Military exercises under FPDA up until today continue to provide for a practicable regional security instrumentality for two Association of Southeast Asian Nations (ASEAN) members, Malaysia and Singapore. By the same token, the FPDA is thereby considered to be "exclusivist" as it does not encompass all members ASEAN. However, the fact that ASEAN has had no appetite for regional military arrangements of its own has meant historic constructs like the FPDA have remained in place. That said, even the long-standing FPDA has from time to time suffered from the vicissitudes of low activity or economic constraints, and Malaysia has been in large part responsible for this. The paper delves into some pertinent issues with respect to Malaysia's foreign policy approach and security stance *vis-à-vis* the FPDA and its continued relevance to Malaysia and the region.

Transitioning from AMDA to FPDA

Malaysia's participation in the FPDA has to be cast in terms of its earlier defence treaty with Britain, namely the 1957 AMDA, whereby Britain and Malaya promised to provide each other with mutual aid in the event of an armed attack on either Malayan or British possessions in the Far East. Article IV of the agreement stated clearly that, "[I]n the event of armed attack against any of the territories or forces of the Federation of Malaya or any of the territories or protectorates of the United Kingdom in the Far East or any of the forces of the United Kingdom within any of those territories or protectorates or within the Federation of Malaya, the governments of the Federation of Malaya and the United Kingdom undertake to cooperate with each other and will take such action as each considers necessary for the purpose of meeting the situation effectively."[2] The two governments were also to consult if the peace of the aforementioned territories was threatened. Should hostilities involving either party occur elsewhere, "the Government of the United Kingdom shall obtain prior agreement of the Government of the Federation of Malaya before committing United Kingdom forces to active operations involving the use of bases in the Federation of Malaya…" Another provision obligated the parties to consult each other "when major changes in the character or deployment of the forces maintained in the Federation...were contemplated". This proviso was designed to ensure that Britain would not introduce nuclear weapons into Malaya without prior approval.[3]

The Malayan Government's objectives in securing AMDA were fairly obvious given the size of its armed forces at the time of independence; it only possessed several battalions of the Malay Royal Regiment, and no air force or navy to speak of.[4] For Britain, the pact was used as a means to protect its national interests in the region with an eye towards its obligations to SEATO. Beneath its formal language, the pact couched a preoccupation with the communist threat to the region. Malaya's long and bitter counter-insurgency campaign against the Communist Party of Malaya, in which the British played the major role, left Malayan policy-makers with the continued perception of the threat of communist expansionism in Southeast Asia.[5] Prior to the signing of AMDA, the ANZAM Agreement of 1949 between Britain, Australia and New Zealand had provided for Malaya's defence.[6] The Commonwealth Far East Strategic Reserve was formed in 1955 and stationed in Malaya, its functions being to contain communist insurrection, provide defence from external attack and carry out SEATO commitments.[7] The protracted negotiations over AMDA saw the exchange of letters until as late as 23 August 1957. According to Dalton, Malaya had evidently "won a maximum of security with a minimum of obligation and it had not compromised on two basic policies of rejecting nuclear weapons and refusing to join SEATO".[8]

In October, AMDA was presented and debated in the Legislative Council. A number of backbenchers, the opposition parties and the trade union representatives continued to oppose the pact, arguing that it compromised Malaya's sovereignty and independence, that military pacts invited military threats and that Malaya was unnecessarily rushing into a military pact without having had a full debate on foreign policy.[9] In winding up the debate, Prime Minister Tunku Abdul Rahman (the Tunku) staked his leadership over the issue, stating "... if the people of this country do not want (the treaty), a simple thing can done and that is — this is all I ask of the people of this country and of my party — to call a meeting, a general meeting, of UMNO [United Malays National Organization] and pass a vote of 'no confidence' against me and my friends and colleagues, and we can just make way for some other clever 'Dicks' to come and run this country". As it turned out, the motion of support for the treaty was unanimously passed, with those opposing it abstaining. In the light of the UMNO and other opposition to AMDA, it is perhaps not at all surprising that Malaya had not joined SEATO. The Malayan leaders dared not hazard a formal tie with the Western bloc even though SEATO was specifically aimed at containing communism, which, presumably, was the presumed purpose of AMDA. Among the other reasons given for non-participation in SEATO was that Malaya would not have gained any military advantage by joining and that the organization was unpopular with India and Indonesia, the two non-communist Asian bulwarks to which Malaysia showed a great degree of deference. The Tunku, when asked about Malaya's decision not to join SEATO, was quoted in Canberra in 1959 as saying: "Well, I don't count, you know. As the representative of my people, I have to do as they want, and SEATO is rather unpopular among my people. I don't know for what reason."[10] A more complete and honest answer would have been that there were strenuous objections from the various segments of Malaysian society to SEATO even beyond UMNO voices, which were surprisingly vociferous. There is a strong suggestion that Chinese groups were also against SEATO and the Tamil Association sent a memorandum to the Tunku on the issue while opposition parties also objected to SEATO membership.[11]

The Tunku himself did not deny the government's indirect links with SEATO. In answer to a question in Parliament, he said: "[A]ll I can say is that we are not in SEATO. In this respect, if SEATO countries are involved in any war, we are not committed to the war, but on the other hand, if Britain entered the war and one of the countries which we are committed to defend, like Singapore, a British territory, or Borneo, is attacked, then we are treaty bound to fight. Perhaps you may say we are indirectly connected with SEATO, but I can say quite openly here and assure the House that we are not in SEATO."[12] ADMA proved crucial in the *Konfrontasi* years, seeing Commonwealth forces doing active duty in Malaysia, particularly in the Borneo state of Sarawak. In three years of conflict with Indonesia (1963–65), 590 Indonesians were killed, 220 wounded and 771 captured. British, Australian and New Zealand casualties included 114 servicemen while Malaysia lost 118 servicemen with 36 civilians killed and 53 wounded.[13]

With the end of *Konfrontasi* and the changes to British East of Suez policy in the late 1960s, negotiations began for the FPDA. By November 1971, this loose consultative alliance was in place. As pointed out by analysts, the *casus foederis* of the FPDA was inferior to that of AMDA. The

FPDA was a loose political consultative framework rather than a collective defence system. The operative clause of the scheme was Article 5 which states "that in the event of any form of armed attack externally organised or supported or the threat of such attack against Malaysia and Singapore" the five governments would immediately consult together for the purpose of deciding what measures should be taken jointly or separately in relation to such attack or threat.[14]

One commentator has suggested that it was based on a "formula that imposed no undue strain or obligation on any party",[15] while another has suggested that while Singapore considered it to be an important component of its defence architecture, Malaysia appeared to progressively devalue it.[16] While there was no requirement for the physical stationing of multinational forces in Malaysia and Singapore, most importantly, the Integrated Air Defence System (IADS) was established at Butterworth Air Base and was headed by an Australian Air Vice Marshall, assisted by a deputy rotating between Malaysian and Singapore.[17] This indicated that Commonwealth links have remained important, if less so, during a transitional period of Malaysian foreign policy. By the mid-1970s, Malaysia had openly espoused and adopted a policy of neutralism and joined the Nonaligned Movement (NAM) by 1974 and this would have important implications for its continued involvement in the FPDA.

The Shift from Defence to Security

Since the 1970s, the evolution of Malaysian foreign policy has seen a shift from strict defence to more broad security-oriented stances and strategies. Malaysia put the final touches to its rapprochement with Indonesia by signing with it, in March 1970, a Friendship Treaty and a Delimitation of Territorial Seas Treaty. The Friendship Treaty was a renewal of a similar treaty signed in 1959, the only such treaty Malaysia has signed with another country. In December 1971, Malaysia and Indonesia, after tripartite consultations with Singapore, announced that "the Straits of Malacca and Singapore are not international straits, while fully recognising their use for international shipping in accordance with the principles of innocent passage."[18] Singapore, while not holding this position, agreed with Malaysia and Indonesia that the safety of navigation was the responsibility of the littoral states and that there was need for tripartite co-operation on the question. The Malaysian-Indonesian position, however, arose from a wish to assert national sovereignty over the Straits. The official view on the extension to 12 miles of territorial seas was that it was necessary for the day-to-day administration of defence and commercial security and that Malaysia was merely falling in line with the majority of nations.

In May 1970, Malaysia served on the three-nation mediation task force (with Indonesia and Japan) to look into the deteriorating war situation in Cambodia.[19] Towards the end of the year, Malaysia attended its first non-aligned nations conference at Lusaka. The event marked Malaysia's acceptance as a "non-aligned" nation. The Deputy Prime Minister, Abdul Razak, led Malaysia's delegation to Lusaka shortly before his succession to the premiership.[20] It was also at the Lusaka Conference that Razak for the first time sought endorsement, at an international forum, for Malaysia's proposal for the neutralization of Southeast Asia. Although the scheme received only partial endorsement at the conference, Malaysia continued to promote it at various international conferences, notably, the commemorative session of the twenty-fifth anniversary of the United Nations in December 1970, and then at the 1971 Commonwealth Conference in Singapore. In his speech at that conference, Razak called for restraint and consideration from the Great Powers in their actions and decisions affecting smaller countries. He called for the neutralization of Southeast Asia — including Vietnam, Laos and Cambodia and which necessitated the endorsement and guarantee of the United States, the Soviet Union and China.

Malaysia's neutralization proposal, while ambitious, was based on a pragmatic appreciation of the Southeast Asian situation. It became the most important of Malaysia's foreign policy strategies in the area of defence and security. The neutralization scheme was subsequently also endorsed in principle by the Commonwealth Conference of Ottawa in August 1973 and the Fourth Non-aligned Summit Conference in Algiers in September 1973. The two Superpowers, America and the USSR, did not respond officially to the scheme while China, verbally expressed support for the idea. The slowness of Great Power response and the feedback particularly from the ASEAN countries led to a slight shift of emphasis in the Malaysian strategy. Increasingly the term "neutralization" was dropped in favour of the expression Zone of Peace, Freedom and Neutrality (ZOPFAN).

The emphasis appeared to have shifted from Great Power guarantees of neutralization to an ASEAN, or Southeast Asian, initiative in fostering neutrality. The concept of neutralization implies Great Power participation, and this did not sit well with some ASEAN countries that would have preferred to have seen the Great Powers disengage from the region. The scheme made limited progress after the Kuala Lumpur Declaration of 1971. By May 1975, during the ASEAN Ministerial Meeting in Kuala Lumpur, it was publicly announced that a "Blueprint for the Zone of Peace, Freedom and Neutrality" was in the process of being formulated by senior ASEAN officials.

This shift in the neutralization strategy was explained in a more comprehensive fashion by foreign policy strategist and then Home Affairs Minister Tan Sri Ghazali Shafie. In a talk on regional security to the Centre for Strategic and International Studies, Jakarta, Ghazali spelled out three types of security issues, namely, internal security issues that arose from internal conflict situations; intra-regional security issues that arose out of intra-regional (Southeast Asian) conflict situations; and external security issues that arose out of extra-regional conflict situations.[21] He argued that these conflict situations could be alleviated by a "Southeast Asian Neutrality System" based on (a) national cohesiveness and resiliency, (b) regional cohesiveness and resiliency and (c) the observance of a policy of equidistance by Southeast Asian states *vis-à-vis* the Great Powers. National resilience refers to a state's "capacity to mobilize (its) population for nation-building and rapid economic development". Regional resilience referred to the ability of each state in the region to be fully committed to its organized international relatedness and interdependence as the first principle of foreign policy. The third element, equidistance, was taken to mean a policy of maintaining non-involved and more or less impartial or neutral relationships with the Great Powers. As Ghazali put it, "In the short term, equidistance reinforces the adoption of a neutral, non-aligned policy stance, which in turn reinforces accommodation between external powers. In the long term, equidistance will entrench a regional policy of neutrality and nonalignment that will facilitate and perpetuate great power disengagement from Southeast Asia."

Seen from the perspective of Malaysia's foreign policy, the neutralization scheme could be viewed simply as a foreign policy strategy grounded on a number of foreign policy objectives. It was not necessarily a concrete or even immediately practicable proposal, and Malaysia's claim to neutrality seemed dubious as long as the FPDA, however loosely framed, remained in force. The change of emphasis in the foreign policy strategy reflected a continual adjustment towards external developments and to some extent domestic events. I would use the terminology of "constructivist strategising" to depict the neutralization scheme. It was an enabling construct for a particular political conjuncture in regional and global politics dovetailing well with a newer set of interests, norms, and ideas nested within the Malaysian political class. By the end of the period, Malaysia had initiated, under ASEAN auspices, a "blueprint" for Southeast Asian neutrality, which, according to a foreign ministry official, enjoyed "90 per cent support" from the other ASEAN countries.

The emphasis on the neutralization of Southeast Asia in Malaysia's foreign policy meant that Kuala Lumpur paid little attention to schemes such as the FPDA in its early years. As noted by analysts Chin Kin Wah and Carlyle Thayer, the more prominent phase of the FPDA came in the 1980s and 1990s. Even so, there were hiccups in Malaysia's participation in these exercises as we shall see in the next section. However, the FPDA's longevity is probably assured given the lack of other regional military arrangements in Southeast Asia. FPDA's most recent exercise, *Bersatu Padu* (United Together), held from 11–29 October 2010, was hosted by the Royal Malaysian Armed Forces (RMAF) and took place at various locations across the South China Sea and on the Malaysian Peninsula. Hailed as a major success, it involved a total of 13 ships, 63 aircraft and about 1,000 personnel from the five countries. The exercise aimed at enhancing interoperability and mutual cooperation among the armed forces of the FPDA nations.[22]

The FPDA and Malaysia-Singapore Relations

In this section, we will examine the FPDA from the perspective of its significance as a CBM for Malaysia and Singapore. This should be understood not just in security and defence terms but in the broader sense of ameliorating an often strained and choppy relationship between the two countries. In spite of a history that was conjoined from the outset, Singapore-Malaysia ties have suffered the vicissitudes of a relationship bounded by too much history and intimacy. At the pinnacle of political convergence was the merger of Singapore with the Federation of Malaya which gave birth to "Malaysia" (with the inclusion of Sarawak and Sabah) on 16 September 1963. At its nadir, the relationship deteriorated into a vicious spiral of irritations over a host of bilateral issues ranging from the denial of sand exports, the use of airspace to the island republic and a territorial dispute over a small atoll.²³ Relations have entered a new phase of cordiality thanks to a leadership change on the Malaysian side in the early 2000s. Two periods in which relations became particularly acrimonious were during the tenures of the premiers Tunku Abdul Rahman and Mahathir Mohamad.

Pedra Branca

The stormy and yet close nature of this bilateral relationship can be illustrated by how the Pulau Batu Puteh/Pedra Branca (PBP/PB) dispute was resolved. The PBP/PB case study provides an interesting example of both confidence building and bilateral socialization which at the same time demonstrated that the process is far from smooth or unproblematic. Even this strictly legal tussle over each country's claim evoked highly emotive responses on both sides. The legal dispute over PBP/PB, a 500 square meters islet which houses the 1851 Horsburgh Lighthouse, dates to the publication of a map by Malaysia in 1979. The issue only surfaced towards the end of the 1980s.²⁴ In mid-1989, Singapore established a radar installation on PBP and as all traffic was banned from the surrounding waters. Malaysian leaders in Johor charged that Malaysian fishermen were being chased away from their traditional fishing grounds. Similar protests were lodged in 1991 when Singapore built a helicopter pad on PBP. At about the same time, on August 9, Singapore's national day, a Malaysia-Indonesia military exercise culminated with the landing of paratroops in southern Johor, codenamed "Total Wipe Out". Taking umbrage, Singapore responded by launching "Operation Trojan" under which its armed forces went on full alert. In an attempt to defuse tensions, in January 1992, Malaysia's Justice Minister said that the dispute would be resolved amicably in the ASEAN spirit. At about this time, two opposition political parties, the Islamic Party of Malaysia (PAS) and Semangat 46 (Spirit of 46) announced that they planned to plant a Malaysian flag on PBP, provoking further protests from Singapore.

In July 1992, Malaysian Foreign Minister Abdullah Badawi stated in Johor that the state should leave it to the federal government to settle the dispute, warning that the alternative to diplomacy was war and that Malaysia did not want to go to war. In September 1994, after a meeting in Langkawi between prime ministers Mahathir and Goh Chok Tong, both sides agreed in principle to refer the issue to the International Court of

Justice (ICJ). The matter lay fallow until 2003 when both countries signed a special agreement referring the dispute to the ICJ for settlement. In May 2007, after the meeting between prime ministers Abdullah Badawi and Lee Hsien Loong, it was announced that the ICJ would arbitrate the case in November 2007. Both countries agreed to abide by the ICJ verdict whichever way it went. The ICJ then sat for 12 days, in the period November 6–23, to hear presentations from legal teams of both countries.[25]

The fact that Malaysia and Singapore agreed to ICJ adjudication in the PBP case after 12 days of hearings at the end of November 2007 was a sign that contentious issues between two countries had been largely ameliorated. On May 23 2008, the ICJ ruled by 12–4 votes to award sovereignty of PBP to Singapore and by 15–1 votes to award ownership of the Middle Rocks to Malaysia. The main contention of the court on Pedra Branca was that "from June 1850 for the whole of the following century or more" the Johor authorities took no action to establish sovereignty over PBP and that Malaysia's maps of 1960s and 1970s also indicate an appreciation that Singapore had sovereignty. In particular, "It is the clearly stated position of the Acting Secretary of the State of Johor in 1953 that Johor did not claim ownership of Pedra Branca/PBP." [26] As for South Ledge, sovereignty was to be decided once the demarcation of the adjoining territorial seas was determined by both parties. The Court said it had not been mandated by the parties to draw the line of delimitation with respect to the territorial waters of Malaysia and Singapore with respect to South Ledge. Spokespersons of Malaysia and Singapore hailed the decision of the ICJ as a win-win situation. As a confidence building measure, the ICJ adjudication no doubt reinforced the ASEAN norms and disposition to resolve territorial disputes by pacific means. This was the second dispute settlement among ASEAN states, the first being the Ligitan-Sipadan settlement between Malaysia and Indonesia in 2002. However, there is no guarantee that the settlement of one territorial issue forecloses the emergence of other bilateral problems. For Malaysia and Singapore, it closed a chapter of poor relations.

FPDA Relationship

Let us now turn to the relationship of Malaysia and Singapore vis-à-vis the FPDA over the years. In theory, the FPDA is based on the notion of "indivisible security" between Malaysia and Singapore. In practice, this is often not the case. We have alluded to how Singapore took umbrage over an Indonesian-Malaysian military exercise in 1991. It is not surprising then that the FPDA at one point or another became a casualty of strained relations between the two countries. For example, this occurred with respect to the holding of the joint military exercises under the FPDA.[27] Such military exercises have been off and on over the years and were stopped during the financial crisis of 1997–98 but even in the good years, military aircraft of one country were not allowed to fly mock attacks against installations of the other. The first bilateral exercises were staged in Sarawak and were on a much smaller scale than exercises between Singapore and Indonesia.[28] In 1990, these low-keyed events were further curtailed on the grounds that "the Malaysian Armed Forces was involved in several similar activities with other countries".[29] In 1997, Malaysia hosted the largest ever FPDA exercise involving 12,000 personnel, 140 aircraft and 35 warships. However, in 1998, at the peak of the financial crisis and during a particularly bad patch in bilateral relations with Singapore, Malaysia pulled out of the STARDEX exercise even as ships from Australia, New Zealand and Britain were steaming towards Singapore. Since 1999 the FPDA exercises have been resumed and have continued, propelled by the post-9/11 political climate.[30]

Malaysia-Singapore differences over the FPDA tend to hinge on the greater value ascribed to it by Singapore. Malaysian spokespersons have from time to time disparaged the scheme, with one deputy defence minister calling it "dead wood".[31] Contrariwise, Lee Kuan Yew's call in 1990 for both countries to allow for open inspection of each other's military capabilities has received no response.

The FPDA's Continuing Relevance

Despite problems, there is little doubt that the FPDA has been of considerable relevance to Malaysia in security from the perspective of its historical Commonwealth ties and its broad security needs. I have also argued that as a CBM, it has been crucial in Malaysia-Singapore relations. While the notion of indivisible defence between the two neighbouring states has arguably been diluted over the years, the broad idea of joint security remains significant. However, there are some clear weaknesses and unresolved thorny issues from the Southeast Asian perspective as pointed out by analysts. First, should the scheme include a sixth Commonwealth member, and ASEAN state, Brunei? Second, how should the scheme relate to other ASEAN states? Indonesia once called for a trilateral defence arrangement among Indonesia, Malaysia and Singapore. Third, should the commander of IADS continue to be Australian? Malaysia had indicated an interest to take over ever since the Australian Mirages were withdrawn from Butterworth. Fourth, should the IADS cover Sabah and Sarawak? Fifth, how can interoperability among the armed forces of the five countries be improved?

The issue of interoperability seems to have received particular attention in recent years. In the FPDA exercise of 2010 in Malaysia, the exercise was indeed aimed at enhancing air, naval and ground interoperability among the five powers. The question of defence partners of the FPDA states also complicates interoperability as these partners do not take part in FPDA exercises. In Malaysia's case, its participation in 2010 for the first time (together with Thailand) in the Rim of the Pacific (RIMPAC) exercise, hosted by the United States, helps to resolve some of the issues of interoperability. RIMPAC is the world's largest maritime military exercise and in 2010 included US allies and partners such as the UK, France, Australia, Canada, Japan, the Netherlands, Colombia, Chile, Peru, South Korea, Indonesia and Singapore. Since 2002, Malaysia has also been party to the Southeast Asia Cooperation Against Terrorism (SEACAT) maritime security exercise.

Some of key points raised by Chin about the fate of the FPDA remain relevant:[32] first, that it could decline as result of a redefining of strategic interests by partners; second, it could become irrelevant if its *casus foederis* is superseded by its new strategic considerations of participating parties; third, it could conversely experience growth and expansion and include new members in the light of changing security contexts. At this point of time, the last prospect remains unlikely but neither does it seem that the FPDA would become irrelevant.

For Malaysia, the FPDA remains a useful instrument in its foreign policy given its shift from strict or conventional defence to maintaining security through more flexible and multi-dimensional mechanisms borne of a broad regional security alignment with ASEAN. The loose consultative character of the FPDA is in synchrony with this shift of Malaysian foreign policy. Many of Malaysia's postures on security issues have dovetailed with its ASEAN policies and commitments. Although the FPDA could be seen to be somewhat in contradiction to this, ASEAN's own reluctance to engage in military arrangements has allowed for Malaysia to maintain historical military links with the Commonwealth and a special relationship with Singapore. Hence the FPDA stands as an important construct in Malaysia's overall security policy and for the promotion of norms of regional conflict management.

Notes

1   Portions of this paper are taken from various chapters of Johan Saravanamuttu, *Malaysia's Foreign Policy, the First Fifty Years: Alignment, Neutralism, Islamism* (Singapore: Institute of Southeast Asian Studies, 2010).

2   Agreement between the Government of the United Kingdom of Great Britain and Northern Ireland and the Government of the Federation of Malaya on External Defence and Mutual Assistance, Signed at Kuala Lumpur, on 12 October 1957 (Kuala Lumpur: Government Printer, 1957).

3   See Robert O. Tilman, 1969, *Malaysian Foreign Policy*, Report RAC-R-62-2 (Washington DC, Strategic Studies Department, 1969) p. 7.

4   According to Jeshurun, the Malayan Armed Forces strength in 1963 was 22,000. The army, known as the Royal Malay Regiment, consisted of seven infantry battalions with one battalion each of Reconnaissance and Artillery. There were plans at that time for the setting up of the 4th Infantry Brigade in the Singapore area. Chandran Jeshurun, *The Growth of the Malaysian Armed Forces, 1963–73.* (Singapore: Institute of Southeast Asian Studies, Occasional Paper No. 35, October 1975) pp. 5-8.

5   For a sustained argument for why it was necessary on the British side to have AMDA, see Archana Sharma, *British Policy Towards Malaysia, 1957–1967* (New Delhi: Radiant Publishers, 1993) pp. 34–54. Sharma saw AMDA as a "convergence of mutual interests" and put down the communist insurgency as a main factor for its signing. For a similar argument from the Malaysian-Singapore perspective, see Chin Kin Wah, *The Defence of Malaysia and Singapore: The Transformation of a Security System, 1957–1971* (Cambridge and New York: Cambridge University Press, 1983).

6   The Anglo-New Zealand-Australia-Malaya agreement was a Commonwealth contingency plan developed after World War Two.

7   See J. B. Dalton, *The Development of Malaysian External Policy, 1957–1963*, Ph. D. Thesis, Oxford University, 1967, p. 64.

8   Ibid., p. 66.

9   See Malaya. Legislative Council, Debates, 2 and 3 October 1957, cols. 3269ff and 31318ff.

10 See Tilman, *Malaysian Foreign Policy*, op. cit., p. 22.

[11] See Khaw Guat Hoon, *Malaysian Policies in South-East Asia, 1957–70: The Search for Security*, Thèse No. 227, Université de Genève (Singapore: Singapore National Printers 1976) pp. 78–79.

[12] See "Legislative Council Debates, 4 session, December 1958, col. 6029" cited in Peter Boyce, *Malaysian and Singapore in Diplomacy* (Sydney: Sydney University Press, 1968) p. 42.

[13] Saravanamuttu, *Malaysia's Foreign Policy, the First Fifty Years*, op. cit., p. 112.

[14] Text of Five Power Defence Agreement, 1971, cited in ibid pp. 159–60.

[15] Khoo How San, "The Five Power Defence Arrangements: If It Ain't Broke...", paper presented as part of the ASEAN Regional Forum's professional development programme for foreign affairs and defence officials held in Brunei Darussalam 23–28 April 2000, <http://www.mindef.gov.sg/safti/pointer/back/journals/2000/Vol26_4/7.htm>.

[16] Chin Kin Wah, 1991, "The Five Power Defence Arrangements: Twenty Years After", *The Pacific Review* 4, no. 3 (1991).

[17] Carlyle A. Thayer, "The Five Power Defence Arrangements: The Quiet Achiever", *Security Challenges* 3, no. 1 (February 2007): 84.

[18] See "Straits of Malacca and Singapore-Joint Statement", *Foreign Affairs Malaysia* 4 (1971): 54.

[19] The participating countries were Australia, Indonesia, Japan, Republic of Korea, Laos, Malaysia, Philippines, Singapore, Thailand and the Republic of Vietnam.

[20] The Lusaka Conference was held from 8–10 September. Tun Razak returned to Malaysia and became prime minister on 22 September.

[21] The points discussed here are taken from Ghazali Shafie, "ASEAN's Response to Security Issues in Southeast Asia", talk delivered at the Centre for Strategic and International Studies during a conference on "Regionalism in Southeast Asia: Problems, Perspectives and Possibilities" in Jakarta, October 1974. Mimeographed handout from the Ministry of Foreign Affairs.

[22] <http://www.chnarmy.com/html/2010-10/6785.html>.

[23] The Pulau Batu Puteh or Pedra Branca claim by both countries was handed over to the ICJ for adjudication in November 2007. The sand ban imposed since 2003 remained in place at the time of writing while the use of airspace, which was curtailed in 1998, was restored in 2001. See K.S. Nathan, "Malaysia: 11 September and the Politics of Incumbency" *Southeast Asian Affairs 2002*, edited by Daljit Singh and Anthony L. Smith (Singapore: Institute of Southeast Asian Studies, 2002) p. 404.

[24] We draw on R. Haller-Trost, *The Territorial Dispute between Indonesia and Malaysia over Pulau Sipadan and Pulau Sipadan in the Celebes Seas: A study in International Law* (Durham: International Boundaries Research Unit, 1995); Harald David, *Tensions within ASEAN: Malaysia and its Neighbours* (University of Hull. Dept.

of South-East Asian Studies, 1996); Andrew T.H. Tan, *Problems and Issues in Malaysia-Singapore Relations* (Canberra: Strategic and Defence Studies Centre, Australian National University, 1997).

[25] The complete proceedings are available at the ICJ webpage <www.icj-cij.org>.

[26] See ICJ Judgment, 23 May 2008, General List, No. 130, p. 75.

[27] The origins of this military arrangement was the East of Suez policy of the British.

[28] David, *Tensions within ASEAN: Malaysia and its Neighbours* , op. cit., p. 82.

[29] At the time, tensions were particularly high between the two countries as Singapore had announced its offer of military facilities to the US in July 1989 without consulting Malaysia.

[30] See Tan, *Problems and Issues in Malaysia-Singapore Relations*, op. cit., p. 72.

[31] Chin, "The Five Power Defence Arrangements: Twenty Years After", op. cit., p. 195.

[32] Ibid., p. 203.

4

The Five Power Defence Arrangements Exercises and Regional Security, 2004–10

Carlyle A. Thayer

The Five Power Defence Agreements (FPDA) came into force in 1971 as a consultative forum and not a treaty alliance. The FPDA was initially conceived as a transitional agreement to provide for the defence of peninsula Malaysia and Singapore until these new states could fend for themselves.[1] The FPDA has evolved and adapted over the past forty years. As the author has argued elsewhere, the FPDA has become "the quiet achiever" and an important component among the plethora of multilateral security organizations making up Southeast Asia's security architecture.[2]

The FPDA has developed a robust consultative structure, complemented by a standing multilateral military component, and a comprehensive exercise programme. The FPDA has gradually expanded its focus from the conventional defence of Malaysian and Singaporean air space, through an annual series of Air Defence Exercises (ADEXs), to large-scale combined and joint military exercises[3] designed to meet emerging conventional and non-conventional security threats extending into the South China Sea. This chapter analyses the contribution of the FPDA's programme of exercises to regional security in the period from 2004 to the present when the latest evolution took place.[4]

Background (1971–2003)

During the first decade of its existence (1971–81), the FPDA conducted only a handful of exercises. It was left up to each member to decide the degree of resources that it would contribute. The FPDA exercise programme evolved slowly. The operational command of FPDA exercises alternated between Malaysia and Singapore.

During the 1980s, the FPDA exercise programme evolved into staging regular land and sea exercises. In 1981, Australia hosted the first land exercise, Exercise PLATYPUS. Since 1981 the FPDA has conducted regular naval exercises. Initially designated Exercise STARFISH, they were renamed Exercise BERSAMA LIMA.

Towards the end of the 1980s, the FPDA exercise programme had become routine and predictable. The FPDA went into the doldrums as the forces committed by external powers began to decline. In 1988, the five defence ministers attended Exercise LIMA BERSATU and took stock of the situation and decided to revitalize the FPDA consultative process. As a result, it was agreed that separate meetings of the chiefs of defence and defence ministers should become permanent and be scheduled every two and three years, respectively.

In March 1990, the defence ministers agreed on policy that provided new direction and impetus for the evolution of the FPDA. The ministers agreed to gradually shift from purely air defence dominated arrangements to combined and joint exercises in which land and naval forces would play a greater role. In 1991, the major ADEX and Exercise STARFISH were held back-to-back.

This evolution of FPDA activities was prompted by several factors. Technological developments and operational doctrine now dictated that attacking hostile aircraft needed to be engaged at greater range from their targets, beyond the ability of ground-based radar. This resulted in the need for air defence capable ships to be added to the ADEX programme and to extend the air space into the South China Sea. This resulted in changes to Exercise STARFISH.

Initially, STARFISH exercises focused on surface ships and submarines with aircraft playing a minor role.[5] Just as ADEX needed surface ships to round out the air defence task, STARFISH required more air power to test the full range of combat capabilities. STARFISH, which focused on maritime defence, began to develop features in common with the ADEX. These separate exercises were brought together and renamed Exercise STARDEX. This new exercise would evolve six year later into Exercise FLYING FISH.

In summary, in the 1990s the FPDA exercise programme of air and maritime defence exercises began to meld and were eventually brought together in STARDEX. For this to occur, the planning process became both combined and joint involving planning staffs from the three armed services of all five FPDA members.[6]

The decade of the 1990s also witnessed the increase in the size of land force exercises. Land exercises were initiated in 1981 but due to Malaysian sensitivities and Singapore's lack of space, they were conducted outside Malaysia and Singapore. Australia and New Zealand alternated hosting duties until 1987 when Malaysia hosted Exercise KRIS SAKTI. Two years later, Singapore hosted Exercise SEA LION. Since 1990, the land exercises have been hosted in rotation with the United Kingdom (UK) portion conducted in Malaysia. Land exercises were given the FPDA codename Exercise SUMAN WARRIOR.

In April 1997, after three years of planning, the FPDA's air and naval components (Major ADEX and STARFISH) were merged into one major exercise, Exercise FLYING FISH. The first FLYING FISH exercise involved 35 ships, 140 aircraft and two submarines. This was the FPDA's first truly combined and joint exercise. Subsequently FLYING FISH exercises were conducted in 2000 and 2003.

In July 2000, the FPDA Defence Ministers met and approved stepping up joint exercises between air, naval and land forces. Importantly, they directed that the Army be more fully integrated in FPDA exercises in order to improve operational capability and interoperability. Army integration into the FPDA's programme of activities required more command post exercises (CPX) and war games to facilitate participation. Land exercises were also integrated with Exercise BERSAMA LIMA.

The fourth meeting of FPDA defence ministers in July 2000 laid the basis for the perhaps the greatest transformation in the history of the FPDA.[7] The Integrated Air Defence System (IADS) was re-designated Integrated

Area Defence to give prominence to joint capability. A long-term plan for joint exercises out to the year 2011 was later adopted.

FPDA Exercises, 2004–11

The FPDA entered a new period of evolution and transformation as a result of ministerial decisions taken in 2003 and 2004. At the fifth FPDA Defence Ministers' Meeting held in Penang in June 2003, the ministers reiterated their commitment to enhancing operational capability and interoperability as a public demonstration of their commitment to regional stability.

The Ministers further agreed that the FPDA should become more relevant by considering options to build on existing cooperation to enhance their individual and collective ability to deal with emerging asymmetric threats. This decision was taken in the context of 9/11 and its aftermath and heightened regional fears of catastrophic terrorist action in the Straits of Malacca.

This was a sensitive matter. The ministers agreed that the FPDA's change of direction should be at a comfortable and sustainable pace, based on sound principles of cooperation that had been developed over the previous years. FPDA exercises then incorporated asymmetric threats with a specific focus on non-conventional challenges such as global terrorism, piracy, protection of exclusive economic zones (EEZs), disaster relief and smuggling of illicit drugs.

In June 2004, the second informal meeting of FPDA Defence Ministers was held in Singapore.[8] The five ministers reiterated the need for the FPDA to adapt to new challenges in the regional security environment, including non-conventional threats. On 7 June, a ministerial statement declared that the FPDA should incorporate "non-conventional threat scenarios such as maritime security serials[9] in scheduled FPDA exercises, and conduct additional exercises focused on maritime security, with the gradual inclusion of non-military agencies in such exercises".[10]

This section reviews five major FPDA exercise series conducted between 2004 and the present, codenamed respectively, Exercise BERSAMA LIMA, Exercise BERSAMA SHIELD, Exercise BERSAMA PADU, Exercise SUMAN WARRIOR, and Exercise SUMAN PROTECTOR (see Appendix 1). All of these exercises were aimed at capacity building, improving interoperability and operational capability. In addition, these FPDA exercises also served to increase military professionalism, develop relationships and mutual understanding in order to promote cooperation.

BERSAMA LIMA is generally conducted annually except when other major exercises are scheduled (see Table 1 below).

TABLE 1
Exercise BERSAMA LIMA

Date	Aircraft	Ships	Submarines	Personnel
2004 Aug 30–Sept 25	60	31	2	3,500
2005 September 5–28	74	26	1	3,000
2008 October 8–24	61	18	—	n.a.
2009 October 5–23	59	20	1	n.a.

BERSAMA LIMA 2004 was the first FPDA "new look" exercise to incorporate both conventional and non-conventional (or asymmetric) threats. BERSAMA LIMA 04 was also the largest FPDA exercise in recent years and was held over 16 days.[11] It included 60 aircraft, 31 ships, two submarines, 3,500 personnel plus ground based air defence, communication support and diving teams. The conventional side of the exercise included a 30 ship task force, commanded by the HMS *Exeter*, testing all aspects of naval warfare and a joint approach to air defence.[12]

BERSAMA LIMA 04 also incorporated a Maritime Interdiction Operation. The main objective of this exercise was to conduct combined and joint operations in a multi-threat scenario involving piracy and the threat of a terrorist attack in the Straits of Malacca and Singapore. Air and naval forces, including tactical teams in fast boats with helicopters, tracked, stopped and boarded a commercial vessel that had been hijacked by terrorists.[13]

The maritime operation was supported on shore by Singapore's new Command and Control facility at Paya Lebar Air Base that interfaced with mobile computer networks to map the "battlefield" with digital infrared cameras.[14] Coordinated naval patrols used improved communications to share intelligence during the surveillance and tracking phases.

BERSAMA LIMA 05 was also designed as a combined and joint exercise in a multi-threat environment involving both conventional and non-conventional scenarios.[15] For example, BERSAMA LIMA 05 included on shore force integration training (including logistics) and live exercises on peninsula Malaysia. The maritime component of BERSAMA LIMA 05 addressed maritime terrorism, protection of EEZs, illegal fishing, anti-smuggling and anti-piracy. At the end of the exercise a total of 448 air missions had been flown and 482 maritime serials completed.[16]

For the first time FPDA military forces interacted with civilian agencies at various stages of the exercise to address non-conventional threats.[17] Civilian agencies included Singapore's Police, Malaysia's Maritime Enforcement Agency, Search and Rescue, the International Red Cross, Petronas and the Malaysian International Shipping Corporation.

BERAMA LIMA was not held in 2006 and 2007. In 2008 BERSAMA LIMA involved operational level planning and tabletop exercises on shore and training at sea. Maritime operations included combined and joint defensive operations including surveillance, replenishment at sea, anti-surface warfare, anti-submarine warfare and strike direction.[18] The warfare serials merged into each other and culminated in all ships participating in a "free play battle".[19]

BERAMA LIMA 09 once again included combined and joint operational exercises in a multi-threat environment. For the first time, the FPDA included a tabletop Humanitarian Assistance/Disaster Relief (HA/DR) exercise to build capacity to deal with a non-conventional security challenges. Participants at the tabletop exercise were directed to discuss actions they would take in given scenarios.[20] On the conventional side, BERAMA LIMA 09 included air combat tactics.

BERSAMA SHIELD is primarily a maritime and air exercise held in the South China Sea that has been held annually since 2004. This exercise allows participants to practice interoperability among all three services in a maritime environment using a range of advanced weapons (such as the AGM-142 missile) with pilots training with and against a variety of aircraft types. This exercise is particularly valuable for Australia, the UK and New Zealand as they gain experience in deploying overseas in a tropical environment.

BERSAMA SHIELD also provides an opportunity for maritime forces to practice interoperability through combined exercises in surveillance, anti-surface warfare, anti-submarine warfare and strike direction.

The most recent BERSAMA SHIELD was conducted from 26 April to 7 May 2010 and involved 59 aircraft, 19 ships, around 2,500 personnel and support elements. This exercise emphasized enhanced interoperability of combined air, ground and naval forces operating over peninsula Malaysia and the South China Sea. For example, eight Royal Australian Air Force (RAAF) F/A-Hornets conducted 98 sorties on tactical reconnaissance, interdiction, and defensive air operations while networked with aircraft and ships from other FPDA participants.[21] During the exercise the RAAF's AP-3C Orions were able to test their upgraded technology against an array of combat aircraft and warships.[22]

Exercise BERSAMA PADU was inaugurated in 2006 and is scheduled to be held every four years (see Table 2). The 2006 exercise was the largest and most complex Command Planning Exercise (CPEX) conducted by the FPDA.[23] The aim of this exercise was to enhance interoperability, operational capacity and mutual cooperation in a multi-threat environment at the tactical and operational levels of warfare.

Exercise BERSAMA PADU 06 consisted of a number of elements including operational level planning, force integration training, logistics, tactical exercises, maritime security exercises and non-combatant evacuation.[24] The maritime security component involved various scenarios related to threats to maritime security including the defence of sea lines of communication (SLOCs), surveillance of merchant shipping and counter-terrorism. The maritime component included simulated conventional battle scenarios and mine laying and recovery.[25] Another maritime scenario involved the interception and boarding of two vessels suspected of involvement in piracy and terrorism.

Exercise BERSAMA PADU 06 also involved land based air defence forces including radar, missile batteries and anti-aircraft guns. In addition, this exercise included logistics staff who rehearsed the proper handling, storage and delivery of supplies. The logistics element was later identified as one of the milestones of BERSAMA PADU.

TABLE 2
Exercise BERSAMA PADU

Date	Aircraft	Ships	Submarines	Personnel
2006 September 5–22	78–86	21–25	1	3,500
2010 October 11–29	66	14	—	3,000

Like previous "new look" exercises BERSAMA PADU involved interaction with civilian agencies. In one scenario involving the interdiction of a ship carrying weapons in the South China Sea, civilian agencies became involved once the ship had been secured.[26] Singapore's Police Coast Guard, Maritime

Ports Authority, Immigration and Checkpoints Authority and Customs were all involved in various phases such as escort and searching the ship once berthed in port. This exercise was aimed at gaining experience in getting aboard a target vessel, securing it and gathering evidence to be used in legal proceedings.[27] Civilian agencies like the International Red Cross were also involved in the non-combatant evacuation exercise.

In 2010, BERSAMA PADU was conducted over the course of three weeks. This was the first time a ship to shore landing was included in an FPDA field training exercise.[28] Malaysian and Australian soldiers, designated the Five Powers Rifle Company, were lodged ashore by naval landing ships. In addition, BERSAMA PADU included air defence operations, including high-end air combat training, air movements, refuelling, and force protection. Combat Service Support was provided in the areas of communications, logistics, and medical and health support.

Exercise SUMAN WARRIOR is an annual land Command Planning Exercise conducted every year from 2004 to 2010 with the exception of 2007 (see Table 3). SUMAN WARRIOR 04 involved a brigade-level combined force as well as the incorporation of air and naval training scenarios. This exercise stressed interoperability and the exchange of professional expertise. The following year SUMAN WARRIOR 05 focused on planning for a non-combat evacuation operation. It was hosted by the UK and held in Kuantan, Malaysia.

SUMAN WARRIOR 06, held in Townsville, Australia involved a CPEX focused on the provision of Combat Service Support (food, water and fuel) for a multi-national brigade on a conventional mission. Participants were grouped into multinational syndicates for a map exercise for sitting a multinational third line Combat Service Support organization. SUMAN WARRIOR 06 was designed to enhance mutual understanding of each participant's organization, equipment and work practices in order to enhance interoperability. SUMAN WARRIOR 08 was hosted by New Zealand at its Burnham Camp. This Command Post Exercise was conducted using computerised simulation of hypothetical scenarios on a war frame system. The CPX focused on the defence of Christchurch and its surrounding area in an asymmetric, non-conventional and complex operational environment. SUMAN WARRIOR 09 was a ten-day map exercise hosted by Malaysia and held in Kota Baharu, Kelantan. It was designed to test the command and control functions of each participant in a simulated environment. This particular exercise was designed to enhance interoperability by testing the planning skills of infantry, armour, artillery, logistics, communication and medical support. Participants were involved in military strategic planning, operations and procedures.

TABLE 3
Exercise SUMAN WARRIOR

Date	Personnel
2004 September 20–October 3	400
2005 September 20–October 4	n.a.
2006 July 3–15	n.a.
2008 September 2–14	500
2009 August 12–19	380–500
2010 November 23–December 2	585

SUMAN WARRIOR 10 was another Command Post Exercise designed to enhance interoperability of a combined force to provide Combat Service Support at the brigade level.

SUMAN PROTECTOR was the final major FPDA exercise conducted during the period under review. It is scheduled to be held every five years. The inaugural SUMAN PROTECTOR was held in 2007 at Royal Malaysian Air Base (RMAF) Butterworth. This exercise combined a large-scale Command Post Exercise with operational air, maritime and land elements in order to enhance combined and joint interoperability

FPDA personnel operated within a Combined Joint Task Force Headquarters alongside air, land and logistics component headquarters to execute a conventional war scenario. The scenario involved the deployment of FPDA forces to Malaysia to contain the imaginary state of Carrano. Carrano was located on Malaysia's southeast border and was determined to invade a large stretch of Malaysian territory. The exercise was designed to contain Carrano through the deployment of an FPDA Task Force.

SUMAN PROTECTOR 07 also involved Civil-Military Cooperation (CIMIC) involving the interaction of the military with government departments and non-government organizations in order to resolve political, legal and media issues. EX SUMAN PROTECTOR 07 involved combat land forces for the first time. During the exercise participants planned and conducted a joint campaign at the operational level in a regional scenario. All military actions were simulated by computer systems. This exercise provided the FPDA land forces the experience of participating in more joint and complex training exercises. SUMAN PROTECTOR 07 was the first step towards developing a full combined joint capability at the operational level. A full field training exercise is scheduled for 2012.

FPDA Exercises and Regional Security

Southeast Asia's strategic environment has altered drastically since 1971 when FPDA was created. Indonesia no longer represents a potential threat to either Singapore or Malaysia.[29] Since the end of the Cold War the probability of conventional state-on-state conflict in Southeast Asia has declined considerably. In the present environment, where the military capabilities of both the Singaporean and Malaysian armed forces have increased both quantitatively and qualitatively, what is the role of the three extra-regional powers? How does the FPDA contribute to regional security?

The FPDA contributes to regional security in six main areas: confidence building; enhanced professional and military cooperation; deterrence against conventional threats; addressing some major non-traditional security threats; individual benefits to each of its members; and spill-over effects to non-FPDA security activities.

First, given the fractious nature of relations between Malaysia and Singapore, the FPDA has served as an effective confidence building measure binding these two nations to continued military cooperation over a four decade period.

Second, the FPDA exercise programme has enhanced professional military skills and contributed to developing military-to-military relations among its members. The FPDA has further demonstrated the efficacy of multilateral training under established arrangements. The FPDA major exercise series contribute to the enhancement of the military capabilities of the Singaporean and Malaysian armed forces across all three services. The multilateral and regional operational interaction at HQ IADS in the design and execution of its exercise programme is unique to the FPDA.

Third, the FPDA contributes to regional security by developing a credible deterrent. The security environment in Southeast Asia has changed since the end of the Cold War. In recent years the military capabilities of other regional states, as well as China's military modernization and transformation, have increased dramatically. As one analyst has noted,

Southeast Asia is experiencing an "arms dynamic" in which states have acquired "stand-off precision strike, long-range airborne and undersea attack, stealth, mobility and expeditionary warfare and, above all, new capabilities when it comes to greatly improved command, control, communications, computing, intelligence, surveillance and reconnaissance (C4ISR) networks".[30]

The FPDA has adjusted its exercise programmes to meet the complexity of the changing regional environment and demands of modern warfare in a maritime setting. In conventional military terms, the FPDA provides a credible deterrent to a potential aggressor. However unlikely the prospect of conventional war, the FPDA posture is defensive and non-threatening. Yet, as this chapter has demonstrated, the FPDA's move towards greater combined joint exercises, coupled with the upgrading of the IADS command and control system means that the armed forces of the five states can effectively operate under a single command.

Fourth, the FPDA contributes to regional security by developing military capacity to address non-traditional security threats. Since the end of the Cold War, Southeast Asian states have identified so-called non-conventional or non-traditional threats as the major challenge to regional security. A quick glance at individual states' submission to the ASEAN Regional Forum's *Annual Security Outlook* reveals that there are a wide number of non-traditional security threats listed but little agreement on the priority to be assigned to each.[31] Many non-traditional security threats are best addressed by non-military institutions such as the police, customs etc.

There are some areas such as piracy and armed robbery at sea, small arms and weapons smuggling, and HA/DR, where the military can play a useful role. FPDA exercises build up capacity and provide techniques for the employment of armed forces to address non-traditional threats based on practical training experience.

Fifth, the FPDA contributes to regional security through the "common but differentiated" benefits each country receives. Both Singapore and Malaysia benefit in strategic terms because the FPDA engages Australia, New Zealand and the United Kingdom in providing security for peninsula Malaysia and Singapore.

All members of the FPDA benefit from the professional experience acquired from FPDA exercises and training activities. Through the FPDA, Malaysia gains access to more capable military platforms, equipment and current operational doctrine which enhances its military capability.

Singapore benefits in a similar manner, but since its forces are among the most modern and capable in the region it is able to develop and test its interoperability in niche areas.

Australia has substantial strategic interests in the stability of the Southeast Asian region and the security of SLOCs. Australia's participation in the FPDA reaffirms its long-term commitment to regional capacity building. The FPDA is an integral part of Australia's regional engagement strategy. The FPDA provides a special channel to enhance bilateral relations with Malaysia and to increase Malaysia's ability to combat threats that may affect Australia's interests such as piracy in Malacca Straits, regional terrorism and people smuggling. The FPDA also provides Australia a forward presence at RMAF Butterworth from which RAAF PC3 Orion aircraft conduct surveillance of the maritime approaches to Australia.

New Zealand has similar strategic interests as Australia in the security of Southeast Asia and its SLOCs. The FPDA affords New Zealand an opportunity to maintain a presence in the region, remain relevant to regional affairs, and make a significant contribution to regional security. The FPDA was specifically mentioned in New Zealand's most recent Defence White Paper released in 2010. The White Paper noted that commitment to the FPDA could involve New Zealand's use of military force and that the FPDA assisted New Zealand in addressing security challenges in its maritime zone.[32]

According to Commander Joint Forces New Zealand, FPDA exercises were "essential for the NZDF [New Zealand Defence Force] to develop procedures and relationships, ensuring the NZDF can work alongside FPDA partners as required. Without joint exercises like Bersama Padu, our defence forces would struggle to work together effectively in a time of need. Bersama Padu gives us exactly the type of training opportunity we need".[33]

The United Kingdom, through membership in the FPDA, is able to further its defence diplomacy and show case its military capabilities in support of British interests including arms sales. Since 2002, the UK's contribution has included a Royal Navy Task Group, Type-42 destroyers, Nimrod Maritime patrol aircraft, Tornado MRCA fighters and deployment of Rapier ground-based air defence missiles systems. Overall UK participation in FPDA exercises has decreased in size and availability of combat assets in recent years and this trend is likely to continue.[34] The UK did not contribute any assets to BERSAMA PADU 10, for example.

The UK prefers the benefits of exercises that address conventional over non-traditional threats. In 2006, the UK noted that FPDA exercises provide valuable, realistic and professional training in war fighting, "training which is difficult for our military forces to obtain elsewhere and the United Kingdom remains committed to significant deployments for FPDA exercises".[35] The UK also noted that although it was willing to explore HA/DR cooperation within FPDA, "it believes focus of the scarce resources available to the FPDA should remain on security issues".

More recently, the UK has reaffirmed its commitment to remain engaged in the region through the FPDA. For example, the Joint Communiqué issued after the third Australia-UK Ministerial Consultations on January 18, 2011 stated:

> The two countries reiterated their commitment to the Five Power Defence Arrangements (FPDA) as a vehicle of practical cooperation and stability in South East Asia. Australia and the UK agreed that a key strength of the FPDA is the ability of the Arrangements to remain relevant to the needs of its members and the strategic circumstances. Both countries undertook to remain engaged in FPDA exercises, within the limitations of their resources, and looked forward to the outcomes of the FPDA Stocktake which will be finalised by the 40th Anniversary of the Arrangements on 1 November 2011.

Sixth, the FPDA contributes to regional security through what might be termed the "spill over" effects of military cooperation to non-FPDA military activities. As noted by the UK's Defence Minister Dr. Liam Fox on 6 June 2010, the FPDA provided a foundation for member states to work to enhance security from assistance to Timor-Leste, natural disaster response, and working together in Afghanistan (where Australia, Singapore and Malaysia have made varying military commitments).[36]

Recent commentary on the FPDA has examined whether it compliments or is being supplanted by the present regional security architecture. One analyst concluded, for example, that the FPDA plays a clear but limited role in the region's architecture.[37] This chapter has sought to demonstrate that the FPDA plays more than a limited role in its contribution to regional security, particularly through the development of conventional capabilities by its Southeast Asian members. Both Malaysia and Singapore are located astride the strategically important straits of Malacca and Singapore which is a crucial chokepoint for navies wishing to transit between the Pacific and Indian Oceans.

The FPDA could become a model for how regional states can cooperate with middle powers in maintaining regional security. Four of the five members of the FPDA are also part of the ASEAN Defence Ministers Meeting Plus (ADMM-Plus) process (Australia, Malaysia, New Zealand, and Singapore). Crucially, Australia and Malaysia are the co-chairs of the ADMM-Plus Expert Working Group on Maritime Security. There appears to be scope — over the fullness of time — for the modalities and operational experiences of the FPDA to be studied, shared and adapted by other ADMM-Plus states.

Appendix 1
FPDA Exercises, 2004–2011

Date	Exercise Name
2004 May	*EX BERSAMA SHIELD*
2004 Aug 30–Sept 25	*EX BERSAMA LIMA*
2004 Sept 20–Oct 3	*EX SUMAN WARRIOR*
2005 March–April	*EX BERSAMA SHIELD*
2005 Sept 5–28	*EX BERSAMA LIMA*
\2005 Sept–Oct	*EX SUMAN WARRIOR*
2006 April	*EX BERSAMA SHIELD*
2006 July 3–15	*EX SUMAN WARRIOR*
2006 Sept 5–22	*EX BERSAMA PADU*
2007 April 23–May 3	*EX BERSAMA SHIELD*
2007Aug 20–Sept 9	*EX SUMAN PROTECTOR*
2008 May 5–17	*EX BERSAMA SHIELD*
2008 September 2–14	*EX SUMAN WARRIOR*
2008 October 8–24	*EX BERSAMA LIMA*
2009 May	*EX BERSAMA SHIELD*
2009 August 12–19	*EX SUMAN WARRIOR*
2009 October 5–23	*EX BERSAMA LIMA*
2010 April 26–May 7	*EX BERSAMA SHIELD*
2010 October 11–29	*EX BERSAMA PADU*
2010 Nov 23–Dec 2	*EX SUMAN WARRIOR*
2011	*EX BERSAMA LIMA*
2012	*EX SUMAN PROTECTOR*

Notes

1   Allan Crowe, *The 5 Power Defence Arrangements* (Kuala Lumpur: Percetakan Konta Sdn Berhad, 2011) p. 3.

2   Carlyle A. Thayer, "The Five Power Defence Arrangements: The Quiet Achiever", *Security Challenges* 3, no. 1 (2007): 79–96; Carlyle A. Thayer, *Southeast Asia: Patterns of Security Cooperation*, ASPI Strategy Report (Canberra: Australian Strategic Policy Institute, 2010), pp. 13–15.

3   Joint refers to military exercises by two or more services (army, navy, air force), combined refers to exercises by the armed forces of two or more states.

4   For recent accounts consult: Damon Bristow, "The Five Power Defence Arrangements: Southeast Asia's Unknown Regional Security Organization", *Contemporary Southeast Asia* 27, no. 1 (2005): 1–20; Gavin Keating, "The Five Power Defence Arrangements: A Case Study in Alliance Longevity", *Australian Defence Force Journal* 170 (2006): 48–61; Craig. A. Snyder, "The Five Power Defence Arrangements (FPDA) in the Contemporary Southeast Asian Maritime Security Environment". Paper Presented to the 49th Annual Convention of the International Studies Association, San Francisco, 26–29 March 2008; Andrew T. H. Tan, "The Five Power Defence Arrangements: The Continuing Relevance", *Contemporary Security Policy* 29, no. 2 (2008): 285–302; and Ralf Emmers, *The Role of the Five Power Defence Arrangements in the Southeast Asian Security Architecture*, RSIS Working Paper No. 195, Singapore: S. Rajaratnam School of International Studies, 20 April 2010.

5   Crowe, *The 5 Power Defence Arrangements*, op. cit., p. 40.

6   Ibid., p. 41.

7   Thayer, *Southeast Asia: Patterns of Security Cooperation*, op. cit., p. 14.

8   "2nd FPDA Defence Ministers' Informal Meeting", MINDEF Singapore, 7 June 2004 and "FPDA nations to practise tackling non-conventional security threats", MINDEF Singapore, 7 June 2004.

9   A serial refers to a part of an exercise. Serials may be numbered. They represent stopping points or stages. Serials may flow or include time jumps to another facet of an exercise.

10 Quoted Bristow, "The Five Power Defence Arrangements", op. cit. Two other FPDA exercises were also held: EX BERSAMA SHIELD (formerly ADEX) and EX SUMAN WARRIOR.

11 Jason Szep, "Asian defence drills to focus on terror threat", Reuters News, 10 September 2004.

12 "HMS Exeter returns from Far East deployment", *Western Morning News*, 4 November 2004.

13 "FPDA to Enhance Capacity in Dealing with Non-Conventional Threats",

Bernama Daily Malaysian News, 10 September 2004 and "Maritime terrorism a top priority for FPDA nations", Channel News Asia, 10 September 2004.

14 Szep, "Asian defence drills to focus on terror threat", op. cit.

15 "Exercise BERSAMA LIMA 2005", MINDEF Singapore, 15 September 2005 and "FPDA nations hold combined exercises", MINDEF Singapore, 16 September 2005.

16 "Bersama Lima Exercise Achieves Its Goal", Bernama, 28 September 2005.

17 "Armed Forces Want More to Take Part in FPDA Exercises", Bernama Daily Malaysian News, 19 September 2005.

18 "HMAS Sirius on Exercise Bersama Lima 08", 28 October 2008, Image Galleries 2008, [Australia] Department of Defence, accessed 11 February 2011.

19 "Sirius gets serious on Bersama Lima", Royal Australian Navy, 7 November 2008, <http://www.navy.gov.au/Sirius_gets_serious_on_Bersama_Lima>, accessed 11 February 2011.

20 "War games include disaster relief exercise", The Straits Times, 10 October 2009.

21 "ADF completes successful multi-lateral exercise", Australian Government, Department of Defence, Defence Media Release, MSPA 158/10, 11 May 2010.

22 "Royal Australian Air Force Takes Part in Exercise Bersama Shield 2010", Australian Government News, 11 May 2010.

23 David Boey, "Current 5-nation war games most complex ever", The Straits Times, 8 September 2006.

24 Jackson Sawatan, "FPDA Countries Conduct Major Air, Sea And Land Exercise", Bernama, 7 September 2006.

25 "Kiwi Forces Deploy to South China Sea", New Zealand Press Association, 4 September 2006.

26 "FPDA kicks off largest and more complex drill", Channel News Asia, 7 September 2006.

27 Marcel Lee Pereira, "Agencies like Red Cross get involved in war games", The Straits Times, 19 September 2006.

28 "ADF to take part in major regional security exercise", [Australia] Defence Media Centre, 11 October 2010.

29 In 1990, Indonesia mischievously suggested the FPDA should be reformed into a three-power defence arrangement comprising Indonesia, Malaysia and Singapore.

30 Richard A. Bitzinger, "A New Arms Race? Explaining Recent Southeast Asian Military Acquisitions", Contemporary Southeast Asia 32, no. 1 (2010): 63–64.

31 Submissions may be found at <http://www.aseanregionalforum.org/Default.aspx?tabid=327>.

32 New Zealand Government, Defence White Paper 2010 (Wellington: Ministry of Defence, November 2010), p. 10.

[33] Government of New Zealand News Release, "Bersama Padu Confirms New Zealand Up to Mark", US Fed News, 21 September 2006.

[34] J.M. Jamaluddin,"FPDA Remains Relevant in Regional Security Structure", *Asian Defence Journal* (October 2010), p. 5.

[35] "Briefing Note on United Kingdom Contribution to the Five Power Defence Arangements [sic]", Department of Defence, Submission No. 26 to Inquiry into Australia's Relationship with Malaysia, Joint Standing Committee on Foreign Affairs Defence and Trade, Foreign Affairs Sub-Committee, Parliament House, Canberra, 17 November 2006.

[36] Zakir Hussain, "UK committed to Five Power Defence pact, says minister", *The Straits Times*, 6 June 2010.

[37] Emmers, *The Role of the Five Power Defence Arrangements in the Southeast Asian Security Architecture*, op. cit.

5

The FPDA's Contribution to Regional Security: The Maritime Dimension

Sam Bateman

FPDA's Evolving Maritime Dimension

Reflecting the maritime nature of Southeast Asia, the Five Power Defence Arrangements (FPDA) has always had a significant maritime security dimension. This has increased over the last fifteen years or so with the greater attention paid both globally and regionally to maritime security. Maritime security has formally been a major concern of the FPDA since the FPDA Defence Ministers' meeting in Singapore in June 2004 when it was agreed that the focus of the Arrangements should be cooperation to meet non-conventional threats in the region, such as terrorism and maritime security.[1]

The initial focus of the FPDA was the air defence of Singapore and Malaysia. This reflected a UK defence policy decision to keep capacity to intervene in the region by air power and bases in Australia and island facilities in the UK Indian Ocean Territory.[2] The focus recognized the fundamental importance of air power in military operations and the pervasive influence of air power on joint operations. However, the navies of the participating countries were often present in a support role in FPDA exercises, and maritime operations have generally been an important element of exercises and other activities conducted under the auspices of FPDA.

During the first decade or so of the existence of FPDA, "only a handful of relatively simple air defence exercises" were conducted,[3] although Royal Australian Navy (RAN), Royal New Zealand Navy (RNZN) and Royal Navy (RN) warships on deployment in Southeast Asia frequently played a role in these exercises.[4] The key element was the Integrated Air Defence System (IADS), including the Royal Australian Air Force (RAAF) Mirage fighter aircraft based in Butterworth in Malaysia. The deployment of warships with an air defence capability acting as "picket ships" in the Straits of Malacca or the South China Sea markedly extended the range at which air defence of the Malay Peninsula might be conducted.[5]

The replacement of Mirage fighters by F/A-18 aircraft in the 1980s led to the Australian decision to move from the permanent basing of fighter aircraft in Malaysia to rotational deployments from Australia. This decision was based on the technical characteristics and capabilities of the F/A-18 making them easier to deploy over long distances, and to the establishment of the major RAAF base at Tindal in the Northern Territory.[6]

Commencing from the late 1970s, the Australian Government encouraged its partners to hold combined multi-national ground force exercises. In 1981 a successful exercise of this type was held in Australia (Exercise PLATYPUS) and another in New Zealand in 1982.[7] At this time, the armies of Malaysia and Singapore possessed relatively greater capability than the navies and air forces, and were able to make a significant contribution to these ground force exercises. However, by the 1990s, Southeast Asian countries were modernizing and improving the quality of their defence forces, particularly their maritime and air forces. From the mid-1990s, FPDA exercises became increasingly more sophisticated and more joint, i.e. involving more than one service from each of the participating countries.[8] Considerable effort between the FPDA partners has gone into the development of mutually agreed procedures and tactics for joint operations.[9]

Naval exercises initially were not a prominent part of the annual FPDA exercise programme. In 1981, the FPDA initiated an annual maritime exercise called Exercise STARFISH.[10] The earlier STARFISH exercises were concentrated on surface naval warfare, but as they evolved over the years, an anti-air warfare (AAW) threat increasingly became an important element. In 1997, the FPDA's air and naval component were merged into one major exercise, Exercise FLYING FISH.[11] FLYING FISH exercises subsequently became quite large with the one in 1989 involving 24 ships, 18 aircraft and 3,000 personnel and incorporating all three dimensions of naval warfare — AAW, anti-submarine warfare (ASW) and anti-surface warfare (ASUW).[12]

Progressively from about the early 1990s, the focus of FPDA activities has shifted much more towards maritime security and maritime exercises. This process was accelerated from about 2000 as greater complexity was added to FPDA exercises and the IADS was restructured from Integrated Air Defence to Integrated Area Defence.[13] An FPDA Minister's Meeting in 2000 recognized that the Arrangements were likely to evolve from mainly air defence to a focus on combined and joint operations.[14] While notionally FPDA major exercises are combined[15] and joint,[16] land operations have progressively become a smaller part of the whole. Table 1 shows that the exercises conducted over the last five years have predominantly been maritime ones. For the last ten years or so, the FPDA exercise programme has been increasingly focused on non-conventional security threats that give priority to maritime security.[17]

Strategic Developments

Several distinct phases in strategic developments in Southeast Asia can be identified that have impacted on the maritime dimension of FPDA and how its members have regarded the Arrangements. The first of these was the initial phase in the 1970s following the establishment of FPDA when the focus was on the security of Malaysia and Singapore mainly against the lingering possibility of a threat from Indonesia, although there were considerations also of bolstering Southeast Asian security against the spread of Soviet influence. The stated purpose of maintaining forces in Southeast Asia during this period was to create a sense of stability so that the Malaysian and Singaporean defence forces, still in their infancy, could develop in a secure atmosphere, particularly their air and naval forces.[18]

The second phase commenced in the late 1970s with increased Soviet activity in the region and in the Indian Ocean. Australia's 1976 Defence White Paper regarded the Soviet build-up of nuclear and conventional arms as the most significant development in strategic circumstances.[19] Major "triggers" for this phase were the Soviet invasion of Afghanistan and the establishment of the Soviet air and naval base at Cam Ranh Bay in Vietnam, both of which occurred in 1979. Australia, New Zealand and the UK were particularly concerned about these developments although Malaysia and Singapore were possibly less so. The first three partners saw the FPDA as an important means of limiting the spread of Soviet influence in the region.

TABLE 1
FPDA Military Exercises 2005–10

Year/Date		Name of Exercise	Type of Exercise
2005	Mar	Bersama Shield 05	Joint/combined air exercise
	Sep	Bersama Lima 05	Joint/combined maritime exercise
	Sep	Suman Warrior 05	Land command post exercise (CPX)
2006	Apr	Bersama Shield 06	Joint/combined air exercise
	Sep	Bersama Padu 06	Joint/combined maritime exercise
	Jul	Suman Warrior 06	Combined land operations exercise
2007	Apr–May	Bersama Shield 07	Joint/combined air exercise
	Aug–Sep	Suman Protector 07	CPX for a joint campaign
2008	May	Bersama Shield 08	Joint/combined air and naval exercise
	Oct	Bersama Lima 08	Joint/combined maritime exercise
	Oct	Suman Warrior	Land exercise
2009	May	Bersama Shield 09	Joint/combined maritime exercise in a multi-threat scenario
	Aug	Suman Warrior 09	Land exercise
	Oct	Bersama Lima 09	Joint/combined maritime exercise
2010	Apr–May	Bersama Shield 10	Joint/combined maritime exercise
	Nov–Dec	Suman Warrior	Land CPX
	Oct	Bersama Padu 10	Joint/combined exercise

Source: Australian Department of Defence, Annual Reports and Singapore Ministry of Defence media releases.

During this period, FPDA was a useful cover for surveillance forces and intelligence agencies of Australia, New Zealand and the UK to monitor the movements of Soviet warships and submarines transiting the Malacca and Singapore straits between the Indian Ocean and Soviet naval bases in the Pacific. It was mainly the need for surveillance of Soviet naval activity that led to the commencement in 1981 of the Operation Gateway patrols of the Bay of Bengal, Malacca Straits and South China Sea by RAAF P3C aircraft based at Butterworth in Malaysia.

While the main concern of the surveillance activities from bases in Southeast Asia was with Soviet activity, Indian naval activities were also of interest due to the close military links during this period between the Soviet Union and India. In a later incident, in 1997, India formally protested to Australia that a RAAF P3 Orion had flown low over the new destroyer INS *Delhi* and dropped sonobuoys near it.[20] This incident, and Gateway patrols generally in the Bay of Bengal, have caused India to have sensitivities to the FPDA that persist to the present day.

The third phase began in the late 1980s with the end of the Cold War, the withdrawal of Soviet forces from Afghanistan, Russia's departure from the Cam Ranh Bay base, and the rundown of Soviet naval forces and deployments through Southeast Asia into the Indian Ocean. Bolstering defence relations with Southeast Asian countries was a key element of Australian defence and foreign policy in the 1980s and 1990s. The 1990s saw a gradual shift in the evolution of the FPDA exercise programme from mainly air defence exercises to combined and joint exercises in which naval and land forces played a greater role. Australia's 2010 Defence White Paper noted that the FPDA Defence Ministers' meeting that year had "reaffirmed the basic purpose of the Arrangements, and recognised their likely evolution from mainly air defence to a combined and joint operational focus".[21]

Most Southeast Asian countries had progressed steadily since the late 1980s in converting their forces from largely ground based forces, optimized for counter-insurgency and internal security operations, to more balanced conventional forces. However, the 1997–98 Asian financial crisis and the need to observe financial stringency led to a marked curtailment of FPDA exercise activity.

The fourth, and second to last, phase began with the terrorist attacks of 11 September 2001 (9/11) in the United States. The October 2001 meeting of FPDA defence chiefs made specific reference to the new threats posed by terrorism, piracy and illegal immigrants.[22] Later incidents, especially the 26 December 2004 Indian Ocean Tsunami, have led to increased FPDA interest in Humanitarian Assistance and Disaster Relief (HA/DR) operations. Operation Gateway patrols were scaled back to about four per year from about 2001 due to operational commitments elsewhere, including in the Middle East and in the northern approaches to Australia following the increase in the number of vessels attempting to enter Australia with refugees.

Following 9/11, perceptions of maritime security have changed. The risks of a terrorist threat to shipping furthered the widening of the concept of maritime security, linking security more closely with safety. This new focus is apparent in the work of the International Maritime Organization (IMO) directed towards making international shipping more secure against maritime terrorist attack. Major measures here are the International Ship and Port Facility Security (ISPS) Code, amendments to the 1988 Convention for the Suppression of Unlawful Acts against the Safety of Maritime Navigation (SUA Convention), as well as the introduction of Automatic Identification Systems (AIS), ship alert systems, and the development of a global system for the long range identification and tracking (LRIT) of ships. At a national level, these developments bring more agencies into play with maritime security. The wider definition of maritime security thus puts a premium on inter-agency coordination; both at the national and regional levels, and to some extent, these considerations have been evident in recent FPDA exercises. This trend has been facilitated by the multi-agency arrangements put in place by Singapore that are discussed later in this paper.

The last decade has seen increased concern in the FPDA for asymmetric threats, particularly piracy, terrorism and to some extent, the proliferation of weapons of mass destruction (WMD). This is in accordance with the global view that the nature of future armed conflict will be much more closely related to the activities of non-State actors, such as terrorists, international criminals and insurgency movements, as well as with the economic and political consequences of failed states.[23] As an expression of concern for the threat of maritime terrorist attacks or the transport by sea of WMD and/or related materials, maritime interdiction exercises were included in Exercise BERSAMA LIMA in 2004, demonstrating the heightened concern of all FPDA members with regional maritime security.[24]

Commencing from the later part of the first decade of the new century, we are seeing a new phase in strategic developments emerging that will impact on the FPDA. This is the shift of maritime power from West to East.[25] China, India and Japan are the rising naval powers of Asia. However, elements of competition are evident in strategic intentions of these three countries, and much of this competition seems likely to be played out in the maritime domain, including in the main area of FPDA operational interest in the Malacca Straits and the South China Sea. Japan has been actively contributing to maritime security in Southeast Asia for the last ten years including with capacity-building assistance to Malaysia and Indonesia, and with providing training opportunities for regional maritime security personnel.[26] The Indian Navy now regularly conducts bilateral exercises with Southeast Asian navies, and China, with more of a "soft power" approach is also offering capacity building assistance to regional countries.

New Maritime Security Measures

With the widening of the scope of maritime security and concerns for the threats of maritime terrorism and the proliferation of WMD, new maritime security measures have been introduced that have changed the face of maritime security cooperation. These include the Proliferation Security Initiative (PSI) and the Global Maritime Partnership (GMP) initiative put forward by the United States, and the Regional Cooperation Agreement on Combating Piracy and Armed Robbery against Ships in Asia (ReCAAP) established by Asian countries. All have had some implications for the maritime dimension of the FPDA.

Proliferation Security Initiative

The PSI involves a set of principles identifying practical steps to interdict shipments of WMD flowing to and from state or non-state actors "of proliferation concern". Frequent exercises are conducted in Asian waters by PSI participants. Many countries have signalled their support for the initiative. Australia, New Zealand, Singapore and the UK all support PSI, but Malaysia does not. However, with Indonesia also not supporting PSI, the US has encountered problems in Southeast Asia with implementing the initiative, including its procedures for intercepting vessels at sea suspected of carrying WMD or related materials.

Global Maritime Partnership

The US has been promoting the GMP initiative as part of its joint maritime strategy.[27] The GMP has two main components: the development of expanded capabilities globally for maritime domain awareness (MDA), and the enhancement of cooperative activities globally and regionally for the provision of good order at sea. MDA is about having greater knowledge of what is going on in a country's maritime approaches and having early warning of a possible suspicious vessel approaching the coast. This awareness makes a major contribution to good order at sea in waters under national jurisdiction, and in the longer term, to good order throughout the oceans of the world. However, the introduction of a global regime for MDA is problematic due to sensitivities about freedoms of navigation; arrangements for access to the data; and the management of the system.[28] Of the FPDA members, Australia, New Zealand, Singapore and the UK are strong supporters of the GMP initiative and MDA while Malaysia is only lukewarm.

ReCAAP

ReCAAP was an initiative of Japan established through meetings of the Heads of Asian Coast Guard Agencies. It has been a significant development for piracy prevention in the region. All ASEAN nations, along with Japan, China, Korea, India, Bangladesh and Sri Lanka, have agreed under ReCAAP to set up an information network and a cooperation regime to prevent piracy and armed robbery against ships in regional waters. It includes the Information Sharing Centre (ISC) in Singapore. Several major shipping countries outside of the Asian region, including Denmark, the Netherlands and Norway, have now joined ReCAAP, but Australia, New Zealand and the UK have not, although it is understood that Australia is seeking membership. However, Malaysia and Indonesia remain outside the agreement. The staff of the ISC includes personnel from many of the ReCAAP member nations. Significantly, the focal points for ReCAAP liaison in the member nations are mainly not navies, but rather coast guards and maritime safety agencies.

Maritime Cooperation in Southeast Asia

Maritime security cooperation in Southeast Asia has advanced enormously over the past decade. This has occurred both between regional nations themselves, and between regional countries and extra-regional ones, particularly with the United States. These developments mean that the value of FPDA as providing unique opportunity for Singapore and Malaysia to gain experience in joint and combined operations has fallen. FPDA exercises have become just one part of a busy annual exercise programme for the navies and air forces of these countries.

Much of the intra-regional maritime cooperation has been to deal with piracy. Piracy in Southeast Asian waters was a major area of concern in the early 2000s, but steady improvement continued until 2009 since when the situation has deteriorated with a marked increase in the number of attack over the past year or so. The situation in Indonesian waters in particular, has deteriorated, especially around the Anambas and Mangkai islands in the southern part of the South China Sea. Very few attacks now occur in the Malacca Straits. The measures taken by regional countries both at sea and onshore have largely been effective in providing security in the Malacca Straits. The Malacca Straits Patrols (MSP), initiated by Indonesia, Malaysia and Singapore, with Thailand joining in 2009, comprises the Malacca Straits Sea Patrol and the "Eyes-in-the-Sky" air patrols are good examples of practical cooperative measures undertaken by regional countries to ensure the security of the Straits of Malacca and Singapore.

The US has become the sponsor of a greater number of maritime exercises in Southeast Asia, both multi-lateral and bilateral, pitched at an increasingly higher level of professional skill and expertise. The Southeast Asia Cooperation against Terrorism (SEACAT) series of exercises is the most significant of these. These exercises effectively take the place of the ill-fated Regional Maritime Security Initiative (RMSI) launched by the US in March 2004.[29] The aim of RMSI was to improve international cooperation, specifically in the Malacca Straits, against transnational threats of terrorism, piracy and trafficking. However, Malaysia and Indonesia were both opposed to the implementation of RMSI in the Malacca Straits. The Chief of the Indonesian Navy, Admiral Slamet Soebijanto, noted at the time that Indonesia would continue to oppose the presence of outsiders, including the US, in providing security in the Malacca Straits and would stick to joint patrol cooperation among the littoral countries, namely Indonesia, Malaysia and Singapore.[30]

The last annual SEACAT exercise was held off Singapore in June 2010.[31] This was a weeklong at-sea exercise designed to highlight the value of information sharing and multinational coordination within a scenario that gives participating navies practical maritime interception training. The Multinational Operations and Exercise Centre (MOEC) on Changi Naval Base served as an information and command centre for the exercise, with liaison officers from the navies and civilian law enforcement agencies of Brunei, Indonesia, Malaysia, the Philippines, Singapore and Thailand.

Singapore and Malaysia have also now participated in the major American Rim of the Pacific (RIMPAC) exercises, which have been held in and around Hawaii every two years since 1971. These are multi-national exercises designed to prepare forces to be interoperable and ready for a wide range of potential combined and joint operations and missions. Singapore first participated in a RIMPAC exercise in 2008, when the Republic of Singapore Navy (RSN) deployed one of its *Formidable*-class frigates, the RSS *Steadfast*, for the exercise. RSS *Supreme*, another *Formidable*-class frigate, participated in RIMPAC 2010 which saw the participation of Singapore and The Netherlands for the second time in a RIMPAC exercise and the participation of Colombia, France, Malaysia and Indonesia for the first time.[32] The other participants in RIMPAC 2010 were Australia, Canada, Chile, Japan, Peru, Republic of Korea and the United States. Malaysia and Indonesia both sent ground force elements to RIMPAC 2010, which included a significant ground forces combat scenario for the first time.[33] RIMPAC exercises traditionally have been based on blue water maritime scenarios.

The Kakadu naval exercises conducted by Australia off Darwin every two or three years also provide an opportunity for bringing together naval and air forces of regional countries. The last Kakadu exercise was held in August–September 2010 with the participation of ships and aircraft from Australia, Japan, Singapore and Thailand.[34] Malaysian naval officers also participated as members of the exercise control staff.

Multi-agency Coordination in Singapore

In the contemporary maritime security environment, countries have to deal with diverse threats that demand greater international cooperation as well as closer domestic interagency collaboration. Singapore has led the way in promoting this cooperation and collaboration. It has established the Changi C2 Centre that enables multi-agency cooperation at home while facilitating greater cooperation and interoperability among international security partners in multilateral exercises and operations.[35] The Changi C2 Centre houses three key entities. First, the Singapore Maritime Security Centre (SMSC) is a one-stop information and response coordination centre to meet the maritime security needs of Singapore. It brings together key maritime agencies such as the RSN, the Maritime and Port Authority (MPA) and the Police Coast Guard (PCG) to work together in one location to enhance situational awareness and improve inter-agency cooperation.

Second, the MOEC is designed to be a conducive venue for militaries, governmental, or non-governmental organization, to interact in the planning and command and control of forces and resources in various operation and exercise settings. The MOEC provides facilities to support the conduct of bilateral and multilateral exercises, such as those held under FPDA, and the Western Pacific Naval Symposium (WPNS). The MOEC can also be used to facilitate international cooperation in areas such as HA/DR. It includes Command & Control Information Systems that enable a shore based Task Force Headquarters to conduct operational planning, and the command & control of maritime operations.

Third, the Information Fusion Centre (IFC) has been established to foster regional cooperation in information sharing among navies and other agencies. The IFC fuses information shared by partner navies and agencies, and shares this across a network of users, heightening the maritime situational awareness of every participant in the network. This helps cue participating countries to take actions to respond to potential threats and developing situations early. Many countries have now posted liaison officers to the IFC, including Australia, France, India, New Zealand and Thailand.

Looking to the Future

When we look to the future of the FPDA, questions must be asked about what Australia, New Zealand and the UK could realistically contribute to regional maritime security under the umbrella of FPDA in the future. We are already well past the stage where there are any credible circumstances in which land forces from these countries might be required, and there must be doubts about the availability and contribution of their naval and air forces. Australia is probably the only one of the non-regional members that could readily contribute naval and air forces in any comprehensive way.

The war-fighting capabilities of the New Zealand Defence Force (NZDF) have been markedly reduced over the past decade. The NZDF could possibly contribute its *Anzac*-class frigates, some P-3 Orion maritime patrol aircraft, and possibly a small land force element to an FPDA mission. The RNZAF no longer has a fighter strike capability, but its P-3 maritime patrol aircraft are being progressively upgraded with more advanced systems to enhance "the ability of New Zealand to contribute more robustly to global efforts."[36]

The British government announced major defence cuts in October 2010 that will lessen the UK's ability to deploy substantial forces overseas.[37] Overall the UK defence budget is to be cut by 8 per cent in real terms over four years.[38] Under these cuts, the Nimrod MRA4 maritime patrol aircraft and the fleet of Harrier jump-jets are to be scrapped; and one of the two helicopter carriers currently in service is also to be laid off.[39] The Royal Navy will retain the two aircraft carriers that are currently being built, but it will see its manpower cut and the number of surface ships falling from 23 to 19. Paradoxically, the greatest capability cuts are in areas that may have had some utility in the FPDA context (i.e. destroyers and frigates, helicopter carriers, maritime patrol aircraft, and short take-off and vertical landing aircraft). As Geoffrey Till has observed, "Britain has already found it difficult to provide the warships and personnel for FPDA exercises", and "may find it more difficult than in the past to provide the augmentees needed to staff FPDA exercises on land and sea".[40]

The FPDA remain important to Australia, and to some extent, New Zealand and the UK as an accepted entry point into the defence and security environment of Southeast Asia. As the 2009 Australian Defence White Paper observed, "we have a deep stake in the security of Southeast Asia... strategically our neighbours in Southeast Asia sit astride our northern approaches through which any hostile forces would have to come in order to substantially project force against Australia".[41] In attending the seventh FPDA Defence Minsters' Meeting in Kuala Lumpur in June 2009, Australia's Minister for Defence reiterated Australia's strong commitment to the FPDA.[42] Despite this reaffirmation of the importance of the FPDA to Australia, the 2009 White Paper makes only a passing reference to the FPDA as "a useful mechanism to confront both traditional and emerging challenges".[43]

Australia's 2009 White Paper does, however, note that "Australia's relationship with Indonesia remains our most important defence relationship in the immediate region."[44] This fits with Australia's commitment under the 2006 Lombok Treaty on security cooperation, which includes maritime security cooperation and capacity building as a significant component.[45] In short, Australia may now attach greater importance to its security relationship to Indonesia than it does to FPDA.

The 2010 New Zealand Defence White paper is rather more enthusiastic about the value of the FPDA than its Australian counterpart of the year before.[46] It identifies the FPDA as New Zealand's most enduring security relationship in Southeast Asia and sees the arrangements as "a valuable anchor for the presence of defence assets in the region".[47] It identifies New Zealand's contribution to FPDA as "a possible circumstance for the use of military force" by New Zealand.[48] In comparison, the 2009 Australian Defence White Paper does not identify an FPDA circumstance as a military contingency in Southeast Asia possibly involving the Australian Defence Force (ADF), but refers more generally to "assisting our Southeast Asian partners to meet external challenges" as a possible military contingency.[49]

Conclusion

It is difficult to avoid the conclusion that FPDA is no longer as important a contributor to regional maritime security as it might have been up until a decade and more ago. Regional maritime security arrangements have developed enormously since the FPDA was established. Other arrangements have become more useful and Singapore and Malaysia do not have the same need for capacity building assistance as was originally the case. The threat perceptions of the FPDA members are very different and in current strategic circumstances, a common operational enterprise is unlikely. A threat to Malaysia and Singapore from Indonesia no longer exists, and the sensitivities of Indonesia to national sovereignty in its territorial sea and archipelagic waters mean an actual operational mission under the umbrella of the FPDA in either the Malacca Straits or the southern part of the South China Sea is unlikely without some involvement of Indonesia. If FPDA is to contribute to maritime security in this part of Southeast Asia in the future, then Indonesia would have to be a partner.

As indicated by the FPDA Defence Ministers' Meeting becoming a triennial event rather than an annual or biennial one,[50] FPDA appears to be declining in strategic importance. The UK, as the FPDA's initial "prime mover", has other commitments and its defence forces are facing severe cuts that will seriously inhibit any future involvement in FPDA exercises or operations. The war-fighting capabilities of the NZDF have declined and any operational commitment by New Zealand to the FPDA would be minimal.

Singapore and Malaysia have established effective cooperative arrangements with Indonesia and Thailand for providing security in the

Malacca Straits. They also participate regularly in maritime exercises and other maritime activities hosted by the United States. Thus the FPDA no longer provides the same unique environment for the professional development and capacity building of the armed forces of Malaysia and Singapore as was the case during the first two decades or so of the existence of the arrangements.

None of this is to say that the FPDA has entirely lost its relevance. The arrangements still offer benefits to the participants but in different ways. They provide a potentially useful operational security link into Southeast Asia for Australia, New Zealand and the United Kingdom. They retain some deterrent value for Singapore. They remain a comfortable cooperative agreement between generally like-minded nations that share a common doctrinal and cultural background in the British armed forces. The defence forces of these nations are able to come together to exercise and develop their tactical doctrine and share practical experiences in an environment that is mainly non-threatening. However, lingering tensions between Malaysia and Singapore are not to be under-estimated despite the undoubted confidence building contribution of the FPDA.[51]

Notes

[1]   Senator the Hon Robert Hill, "Key Step by FPDA to tackle Regional Terrorism", *Media Release 107/2004*, 7 June 2004.

[2]   I.M. Cumpston, *Australia's Defence Policy 1901–2000*, Vol. 2 (Canberra: I.M. Cumpston, 2001), p. 213.

[3]   Carlyle A. Thayer, "The Five Power Defence Arrangements: The Quiet Achiever", *Security Challenges* 3, no. 1 (February 2007): 84.

[4]   The author himself participated in such an exercise while serving in the frigate HMAS *Parramatta* in 1971.

[5]   A picket ship is a warship equipped with long range air warning radars used to increase the radar detection range around a vulnerable target to protect it from surprise attack. The ship will usually have a fighter control capability to allow it to direct the interception of incoming enemy aircraft by friendly fighters. An airborne early warning (AEW) aircraft has a similar role.

[6]   Cumpston, *Australia's Defence Policy*, op. cit., p. 244.

[7]   Ibid., p. 219.

[8]   Ibid., p. 288.

[9]   Commonwealth of Australia, *Australian Maritime Doctrine: RAN Doctrine — 2010*, 2nd ed. (Canberra: Sea Power Centre — Australia, 2010), p. 20.

10   Thayer, "The Five Power Defence Arrangements", op. cit., p. 85.

11   Ibid., p. 87.

12   Ibid., p. 86.

13   Chin Kin Wah, "Singapore's Perspective on the Asia-Pacific Security Architecture", Chapter 10 in *Asia-Pacific Security Cooperation — National Interests and Regional Order"* edited by See Seng Tan and Amitav Acharya (New York: M. E. Sharpe, 2004), p. 176 .

14   Cumpston, *Australia's Defence Policy*, op. cit., p. 325.

15   A combined operation is one conducted by forces of two or more allied nations acting together for the accomplishment of a single mission. Commonwealth of Australia, *Australian Maritime Doctrine*, p. 187.

16   Joint connotes activities, operations, organizations, etc in which elements of more than one Service of the same nation participate. Ibid., p. 197.

17   Thayer, "The Five Power Defence Arrangements", op. cit., p. 89.

18   Air Marshall David Evans, *A Fatal Rivalry — Australia's Defence at Risk* (South Melbourne: MacMillan Australia, 1990), p. 12.

19   Cumpston, *Australia's Defence Policy*, op. cit., p. 191.

20   Brendan Nicholson, "How we spy on our friends", *The Sunday Age*, 8 April 2001.

21   Commonwealth of Australia, *Defence 2000 — Our Future Defence Force* (Canberra: Department of Defence, 2000), p. 40, para. 5.38.

22   Chin Kin Wah, "Singapore's Perspective", op. cit., p. 176.

23   Commonwealth of Australia, *Australian Maritime Doctrine: RAN Doctrine — 2010*, 2nd ed. (Canberra: Sea Power Centre — Australia, 2010), p. 68.

24   Chris Rahman, "The International Politics of Combating Piracy in Southeast Asia" in *Violence at Sea: Piracy in the Age of Global Terrorism* edited by Peter Lehr (Abingdon: Routledge, 2007), p. 196.

25   Geoffrey Till, "Asia Rising and the Maritime Decline of the West: A Review of the Issues", *RSIS Working Paper No. 205*, 29 July 2010.

26   Richard J. Samuels, "New Fighting Power: Japan's Growing Maritime Capabilities and East Asian Security", *International Security* 32, no. 3 (Winter 2007/08): 84–112.

27   US Navy, US Marine Corps and US Coast Guard, "A Cooperative Strategy for Twenty-first Century Seapower", October 2007, <www.navy.mil/maritime/MaritimeStrategy.pdf>.

28   Sam Bateman, "Navies and the Maintenance of Good Order in Peacetime", in *The Politics of Maritime Power — A Survey* edited by Andrew T. H. Tan (Abingdon: Routledge, 2007), p. 107.

29   The first mention of the RMSI was in an address by ADM Tom Fargo USN, Commander, US Pacific Command, to the US Congress in March 2004. Joshua Ho, "Operationalising the Regional Maritime Security Initiative", *IDSS*

Commentaries 18/2004 (Singapore: Institute of Defence and Strategic Studies, 27 May 2004).

30 "Indonesian navy rejects US presence in Malacca Straits", Vietnam News Agency, 27 October 2005 (http://www.vnagency.com.vn/NewsA.asp?LANGUAGE_ID=2&CATEGORY_ID=33&NEWS_ID=172313) (accessed on 1 November, 2005).

31 Ensign Jason S. Fischer USN, "SEACAT Exercise Kicks Off in Singapore", *Commander U.S. Seventh Fleet Press Release*, 21 June 2010, <http://www.c7f.navy.mil/news/2010/06-june/34.htm>.

32 Ministry of Defence, Singapore, *About RIMPAC*, 23 August 2010, <http://www.mindef.gov.sg/imindef/mindef_websites/topics/exrimpac/abt_rimpac.html>.

33 Gidget Fuentes, "Sea-based artillery doctrine tested at RIMPAC", *Marine Corps Times*, 24 July 2010, <http://www.marinecorpstimes.com/news/2010/07/marine_rimpac_072410w/>.

34 "Exercise Kakadu 2010 draws to a close", *Defence News*, 3 September 2010, <http://www.defence.gov.au/defencenews/articles/0903/0903.htm>.

35 Sam Bateman, Joshua Ho and Jane Chan, *Good Order at Sea in Southeast Asia*, RSIS Policy Paper (Singapore: S. Rajaratnam School of International Studies, May 2009), p. 33.

36 New Zealand Government, *Defence White Paper 2010* (Wellington: Ministry of Defence, 2010), para. 5.39, p. 53.

37 James Kirkup and Thomas Harding, "Defence review: cuts will leave Britain unable to fight wars like Iraq and Afghanistan", *The Telegraph*, 20 October 2010.

38 Ibid.

39 Kim Sengupta and Nigel Morris, "Forces left unable to launch 'major' missions overseas", *The Independent*, 20 October 2010.

40 Geoffrey Till, "Britain's Future Defence: Impact on FPDA", *RSIS Commentary 145/2010*, 10 November 2010.

41 Australian Government, *Defending Australia in the Asia-Pacific century: Force 2030* (Defence White Paper, Canberra: Department of Defence, 2009), para. 5.12, pp. 42–43.

42 The Hon. Joel Fitzgibbon, Minister for Defence, "Minister for Defence attends Foreign Defence Ministers Meeting in Malaysia", *Media Release 102/2009*, 1 June 2009.

43 Australian Government, *Defending Australia*, op. cit., para. 11.24, p. 97.

44 Ibid., para. 11.21, p. 96.

45 Chris Rahman, "Australia and Maritime Security in the Northeast Indian Ocean", in *ASEAN India Australia — Towards Closer Engagement in a New Asia*

edited by William T. Tow and Chin Kin Wah (Singapore: Institute of Southeast Asian Studies, 2009), p. 195.

[46] Sam Bateman, "Coming Back to the US Fold: New Zealand Defence and Security Policies", *RSIS Commentary 146/2010*, 10 November 2010.

[47] New Zealand Government, *Defence White Paper 2010*, op. cit., para. 3.51, p. 30.

[48] Ibid., para 2.6, p. 16.

[49] Australian Government, *Defending Australia*, op. cit., para. 7.13, p. 55.

[50] Rahman, "Australia and Maritime Security", op. cit., p. 210.

[51] Thayer, "The Five Power Defence Arrangements", op. cit., p. 92.

6

An FPDA Role in Humanitarian Assistance and Disaster Relief?: It's More than Just the Armed Forces

Jim Rolfe

The role of armed forces in Humanitarian Assistance and Disaster Relief (HA/DR) is highly relevant for several reasons. The first is due to the increasing salience of HA/DR issues in the Asia Pacific, especially given the extreme propensity the region has for natural disasters and the extent of urban agglomerations, both of which mean that the scale of disaster is likely to be large and to require all available resources to respond. Given this, it makes sense for regional armed forces to examine how they can contribute effectively when called upon. The second reason, directly relevant to the Five Power Defence Arrangements (FPDA), is because FPDA ministers have called for an examination of the issue and its applicability for the armed forces of member states. The call is not surprising given the first point and the fact that the FPDA as an institution has always been prepared to evolve to meet the needs of a changing geopolitical and operational environment.

In examining HA/DR issues, the FPDA is following a now relatively common line which sees ever more consideration of the use of armed forces in non-traditional, non-war fighting roles. In 2008, the Stockholm International Peace Research Institute (SIPRI) published a study of the effectiveness of the armed forces in disaster response. Two years later the UK-based international conference centre Wilton Park ran a disaster management conference with a session dealing with the role of armed forces in disaster risk reduction, (an HA/DR issue). Both the ASEAN Regional Forum and the ASEAN Defence Ministers' Meeting Plus (ADMM-Plus) have begun to consider how HA/DR issues might be incorporated into military activities and capabilities, and the Western Pacific Naval Symposium devoted its 2011 session to HA/DR issues. Nonetheless, merely because the issue is salient is not in itself a sufficient reason for the FPDA to undertake tasks in this area; it is though a reason for a more systematic examination of the relevant factors.

Despite the international interest, HA/DR concepts are still relatively new ground for most armed forces. This does not mean that armed forces have not in the past responded, and responded well, when called up to provide disaster relief: they have. It does mean, however, that armed forces generally have not examined the concept of disaster management in any systematic way. Instead, there has been an assumption that if the armed forces are good at their conventional role then they can probably take on a disaster relief role when called upon. This is not necessarily the case and is reminiscent of the attitude to peace keeping operations (PKOs) held by many armed forces until the 1990s from which time the number, range and complexity of PKOs increased dramatically, and thinking about and studying the issues increased commensurately.

There are positions held by many in the armed forces and outside them about the use of the military in these non-traditional roles. Broadly, they are around the theme that armed forces should not be involved in disaster management except in emergencies and at the margins, of which more later. Suffice it to say that armed forces have potentially both a humanitarian response role and a longer-term developmental role in disaster management.

This chapter focuses on two areas. First, it examines the general considerations surrounding the use of armed forces in disaster management; an issue not generally at the forefront of military analysis although the recent spate of conferences and analysis indicates that that might be changing. Secondly, it addresses what specifically the FPDA might have to consider if it were to formally develop a significant role in disaster management. Both components of the analysis are important, but the FPDA can not be effective in disaster management, and should not attempt to develop a disaster management role, without a careful analysis of the background context laid out in the first part of the chapter.

The FPDA and New Issues

Although the FPDA's history is not the topic of this paper, there is one point that is worth emphasising. The organization is an example of evolution in practice through its history of adaptation as it has sought to remain relevant to the international environment and the current needs and preoccupations of its members. That adaptive capacity means that the organization is probably capable of successfully taking on a new non-conventional role if that is called for. But it does not mean that the FPDA should necessarily take on such a role.

Originally the FPDA was established as a means for ensuring the defence of the Malay Peninsula by keeping Australia, New Zealand and the United Kingdom engaged in a systematic and committed way. Since then, the grouping has evolved considerably. Formal defence against conventional attack, although still a focus, is not a significant security concern for the members. The regional air defence system has developed into an area defence system that oversees a range of complex exercises designed to ensure the ability of the national armed forces to work together. In 2004 maritime terrorism was added to the organization's agenda and the issue was addressed through a multinational exercise. Given events since then, that could be seen as prescient. Since 2003 non-conventional activities have been one focus for the group, with HA/DR coming on to the agenda in 2006 with the suggestion that the partners could establish a coordinating centre for humanitarian and relief operations.[1]

The Context of Disaster Management Activities

There is a conceptual difference between humanitarian assistance and disaster relief in that humanitarian assistance can be applied in and following both conflict and natural disasters whereas disaster relief is, almost by definition, applied following natural disasters (which may, of course, occur in a conflict or post-conflict area). In this chapter I restrict the discussion to the circumstances surrounding natural disasters, although many of the principles and concepts are identical or overlap considerably.

There is a clear need for HA/DR capacity within the region. The Asia Pacific is a region of disaster. Some 40 per cent of the world's disasters between 2000 and 2008 occurred in the region. In that period the regional disasters affected more than 100 million people, killed more than 233,000 and caused about US$103bn in damage. These figures represented some 87 per cent of the total economic effects and 99 per cent of deaths from natural disasters globally.[2]

Given the need, if the armed forces are going to be involved in HA/DR they must understand the context within which international disaster management conventions work. This is an essential pre-requisite for the development of comprehensive and effective operational capabilities of the kind envisaged for the FPDA since the subject's first appearance on its agenda in 2006.

Although states and their armed forces responding to natural disasters naturally choose their responses in those areas where they have current capacity, this inclination might be problematic because of the integrated nature of the international disaster management framework. The basic principles are contained in the so-called Hyogo Framework which is intended to ensure, among other outcomes, that states become more resilient to the threat of natural disasters.[3]

Hyogo calls for the systematic incorporation of risk reduction approaches into the design and implementation of emergency preparedness, response and recovery programmes and in the reconstruction of affected communities. Priorities for action include the need to strengthen disaster preparedness for effective response at all levels. Key components include requirements to "support the creation and strengthening of national integrated disaster risk reduction mechanisms" and to ensure "authorities, individuals and communities in hazard-prone areas are well prepared and ready to act and are equipped with the knowledge and capacities for effective disaster management" so that in times of disaster, impacts and losses can be substantially reduced.

Internationally, there is widespread agreement on the need for the closer integration of disaster relief, rehabilitation and development. This implies a longer-term perspective behind post-disaster action, whether immediate response or longer-term recovery. In essence it means that relief and rehabilitation efforts should contribute to long-term development and the reduction of vulnerability. Wherever possible relief and rehabilitation should not simply reconstruct the existing risk.[4]

The implication of all this is that if armed forces are to be involved in disaster operations they need to be conversant with the context within which they are operating. This is to ensure that military activities do not inadvertently compromise disaster management actions being undertaken by other agencies conforming to Hyogo, to ensure that post-disaster relief activities are developed with an understanding of longer-term risk reduction needs and to ensure that military participants understand the context within which other relief agencies are operating. The military response needs to take the civil environment into account and conversely, civil actors will need to work with armed forces in ways that might not be familiar to them.

The Armed Forces and Disaster Management

For a range of reasons, there are sections of the international community (both within the government and in the non-government sector) that are at best suspicious of the activities of armed forces in any context other than armed conflict and at the extreme reject absolutely any role for the armed forces in disaster management generally and even in disaster relief specifically. For disaster relief, mainstream opinion allows for military response under agreed guidelines, although again there is reluctance in some sectors for the armed forces to have any more than an immediate "in and out' response role. A summary of mainstream opinion might be as put in a recent SIPRI report: "...while humanitarian relief is and should remain a predominantly civilian function, foreign military assets can play a valuable role in natural disaster relief. Significant problems and questions remain regarding their deployment, but foreign military assets are almost certain to remain a common feature of major international disaster relief operations."[5]

There are many issues surrounding the use of the armed forces in development, humanitarian and disaster relief roles, all of which are inter-related. There is a concern by some that the armed forces will eclipse the state that it ostensibly serves by overstepping the boundaries of constructive activity and thus blurring the lines between defence, development and commercial self-interest.[6] This, in the eyes of many in the humanitarian and development communities, can and will lead to confusion as to the relationship between the military and the NGO sector to the detriment of the latter. At its extreme, if the principle of distinction between military and civilian action is lost the consequences are seen as being potentially dire. As one NGO notes: "When a social or humanitarian programme depends on the Armed Forces, it involves the population in armed conflict".[7]

The so-called Oslo Guidelines are at the basis of most commentary.[8] The guidelines "establish the basic framework for formalizing and improving the effectiveness and efficiency of the use of foreign military and civil defence assets in international disaster relief operations".[9] In the Asia-Pacific region the guidelines were examined by the ARF in a 2009 seminar which noted that "militaries played different roles in HADR operations in different countries — in some countries the militaries were the main institution while, in others, it was the civil agencies that took the lead with the militaries play a supporting and complementary roles".[10] The seminar concluded that there was a need for an "overarching framework for HADR cooperation that was capable of reconciling international and regional laws on disaster relief assistance".[11]

NGOs such as Oxfam support the Oslo Guidelines with the view that "military assets should only be used as a last resort, where there is no civilian alternative and only the use of military assets can meet a critical humanitarian need".[12] Reinforcing this approach, one recent analysis of the armed forces' role in Disaster Risk Reduction (DRR: a component of the overall disaster management framework) discusses DRR in terms of "last resort" and "exceptional circumstances".[13]

These are not unanimous or uncontested positions. For some, the armed forces are considered as having "a stake in DRR policy".[14] In line with that view, in most countries armed forces personnel, equipment and facilities are called upon to support emergency services during major disasters. In some they may take the leading role, especially if civil authorities are overwhelmed, as in the case of the Dominican Republic following Hurricane George in 1998.[15]

Within the Asia Pacific, these issues are less problematic: "the importance of civil-military cooperation in disaster relief" is highlighted.[16] Indeed, some authorities go further and argue that there is a "need to see humanitarian relief as a core military task" and "the need to create better relationships between civilian and military agencies where humanitarian assistance is concerned".[17]

Within the FPDA's region then, humanitarian responses by the armed forces to disaster are almost a given. The fact of this has been recognised in the 2005 ASEAN Agreement on Disaster Management and Emergency Response and institutionalized through the Asia Pacific Conference on Military Assistance to Disaster Response Operations process.[18] Between them, these arrangements emphasize state sovereignty but also legitimize the role of the armed forces in disaster response and move the debate from "should they be used" to "how best can they be used", with the overall caveat that foreign military assets "will normally be used when there is no comparable civilian alternative assistance available at the time and location needed and when only the use of military or civil defence assets can meet a critical humanitarian need".[19] Not an onerous restriction in a region in which natural disasters tend to be devastating and to overwhelm any local capacity to respond.

In more operational terms, the 2010 ADMM-Plus agreed "on the importance of deepening cooperation in humanitarian assistance and disaster relief" and welcomed "existing initiatives to build capacity and enhance capabilities, including the ARF Disaster Relief Exercise and ASEAN HADR Table-top exercise in 2011".[20] These activities were designed to portray the integrated civil and military environment for HA/DR activities.

Armed Forces Responses

We understand that the armed forces do not routinely prepare themselves for a role in the aftermath of natural disasters. Following flooding in Australia in 2011, a senior military officer observed: "We don't position ourselves specifically to respond to natural disasters, but then again, our general level of readiness and our agility allows us to respond quickly to any requests".[21]

There are good reasons for accepting a role for the armed forces in this area. They have evident strengths for the role. Some of these strengths include the ability to gather together and move resources (both personnel and materiel) at short notice. This is an extremely important capability given the emphasis on the likelihood of survivors being found reduces dramatically after the first 100 hours following a disaster. As well, armed forces have a culture that emphasizes training and preparedness. This should mean, if they utilize their training resources to prepare for a disaster role, that they are capable of operating effectively within the wider disaster management system. The armed forces also have specific operational capabilities that lend themselves directly to undertaking technical assessments of damaged or suspect infrastructure following a natural disaster. For example, Royal Australian Navy minehunting vessels cleared shipping channels in the Brisbane River following extreme flooding there in 2011, a capacity not found in the civil sector. Finally, and obviously, the armed forces have the ability to use force if that should become necessary.[22]

These capabilities lead to some obvious areas in which the armed forces could, depending on national or international needs, work in disaster management. These may be grouped around headings such as: response; training; national capacity building for disaster response and risk reduction; and at the extreme, reinforce and support police forces to prevent or respond to a breakdown in law and order. These are almost certainly not controversial but nor, generally, are they mainstream military activity. Training for disaster response, for example, is not a major component of military activity in most states and while the development of national capacities (through, for example, infrastructure expansion activities) is a task for some regional armed forces, it is an open question as to whether such activities take the disaster resilience requirements of the Hyogo Framework into account.

The most common use for the armed forces is in short-notice response to disaster. But being able to respond at short notice is probably not sufficient if response is seen as being integrated within a wider disaster management framework. If the armed forces are going to be effective in disaster operations in the areas identified above, or in others, they need to understand the concept and its complexities.[23] These include: understanding the detail of the disaster management framework; understanding of the roles, the capabilities and the limitations of all actors; understanding that other actors do not necessarily work like the armed forces and do not necessarily want to; and understanding that the armed forces are generally supporting rather than leading disaster relief and humanitarian activities.

Taking these points into account, some general prescriptions for involving the armed forces in HA/DR may be derived. These include, most importantly, the need to ensure that disaster management activities undertaken by the armed forces conform to international agreements, conventions and agreed principles. Therefore, disaster management best practice needs to be a component of all relief activity. United Nations' prescriptions might be a start, although they are not aimed directly at the armed forces.[24] This, if taken to a logical conclusion, is all likely to require armed forces to direct resources to these activities at the expense of what might be considered core activities. There must, therefore, if this approach is followed, be a clear understanding that the benefits received from armed forces interventions are greater than the costs — both transactional and opportunity.

If armed forces are going to be involved in disaster management on more than an *ad hoc* basis, the full range of the issues need to be socialised throughout not only those elements of the armed forces involved or likely to be involved in disaster management, but also within higher command levels to ensure that disaster management preparation is not diverted to traditional "core military activity", or to frame the issue slightly differently in line with the position of the New Zealand Minister of Defence cited earlier, to ensure that disaster management preparation is made a core military activity.

Any participant in disaster management needs an understanding of the capacities and limitations of all other actors and an understanding of where the armed forces fit into whole of government, whole of nation and whole of community efforts. Any time a force intervenes within another community it must have an understanding of the needs and cultural requirements of the affected community and of other actors, such as NGOs and other civil agencies, involved in disaster management. This includes, for example, the requirement to be able to communicate with both the recipient and disaster management communities in the community's language and with an understanding of community perspectives.[25] This in itself can be a significant training burden.

Issues for the FPDA

Even if it is accepted that national armed forces have a role in disaster management, there are questions for the FPDA. In outline only, these might include such policy questions as, for example, should the FPDA become involved in disaster management as an organization? If so, will the FPDA work as an FPDA grouping or as a set of national contributions with a common doctrine and an assumption that they will group on an *ad hoc* basis when appropriate? But if this approach is taken, what of the moves within ASEAN for member states' armed forces to work together more closely? Malaysia and Singapore are members of both groupings and Australia and New Zealand are associated through the ARF and ADMM-Plus.

There are questions of utility. Can the FPDA add value to international efforts by developing an organizational (as opposed to national) capacity to work in the HA/DR sphere? Possibly it can, but more work needs to be done in determining that before decisions about moving to operational or even a general cooperative arrangements are made.

There are skill-related questions. If disaster management is to be carried out in accordance with international agreements, and if specific capacities to conduct disaster operations are to be developed, the relationship between war-fighting skills and non-traditional skills within those elements of national armed forces relevant to FPDA need to be addressed. Questions that member states and the organization itself need to answer are around "either/or" or "both/and" for the range of skills. Few would argue that the only role today for the armed forces lies in these non-traditional roles, but some argue that there is no, or only a very limited, role and that the armed forces must prepare for conflict rather than for activities which are seen as peripheral.[26] Probably, most will accept some form of "both/and" approach, but that still leaves questions about the balance between preparing for disaster activities and for operational roles in armed conflict.

If the FPDA states choose to develop a disaster capacity, process-based questions become important. For example, whether member states will specialize in different aspects of disaster management or whether each state will work out its own approaches. It could be, for example, that one member state becomes responsible for training (including with the whole range of natural disaster actors), another for developing legal frameworks, another for logistics and another command, control and coordination. All of this presupposes a common operational doctrine. That being the case, what doctrinal approaches will be adopted and how will they be developed? Doctrinal responses have to be around questions of roles, relationships, responsibilities and process for the armed forces.

Questions of opportunity and transaction costs will have to be considered. If military resources are utilized in this area there is an absolute cost and the question must be asked whether other, perhaps more specialized, agencies could do the job more cheaply. Also, if military resources are diverted to this non-warfighting role, what of the true military capabilities? What should be the balance between state protection in the military sense and state protection in the more social sense? These are difficult questions that need to be posed and answered.

Finally, in this analysis but undoubtedly not the last word, the FPDA will have to work out how relations with the civil sector will be developed.

This is not just with the humanitarian sector, although that is extremely important, but also national agencies (aid, disaster management, diplomatic, police) with a legitimate and in most cases a longer-standing and deeper role in disaster management than that held by the armed forces.

The Way Ahead

The forgoing discussion has established that humanitarian assistance and disaster relief are a component of a wider disaster management system which is integrated and the components of which are interdependent and that is governed by international agreements. It has also established that there is a legitimate role for the armed forces, although that role is surrounded by rules and norms which are not necessarily well-known to the armed forces. Finally, by implication, if the armed forces are to be fully effective in disaster management activities, including narrow disaster relief and response, they need to have a complete understanding of the issues surrounding disaster management. All this comes under the general heading of "ensuring readiness through prior planning". This is easy to assert, but much harder to achieve in practice.

So that outcomes in this area can be optimised, armed forces can not just assume that if they turn up with what they have, the problems will be solved. In the short term some problems may be resolved, but possibly at the expense of unsustainable solutions that degrade longer-term outcomes for disaster risk reduction.

The FPDA needs to decide what it wants to do within the disaster management sphere. That decision needs to be made with an understanding of the interdependence of the disaster management system and that skills in disaster management might take away from war-fighting skills. If the decision to develop an organizational capacity is made, there will be a considerable period of development (taking at least several years) before any significant group capacity will be developed. None of these decisions can be taken without considerable analysis of the issues. This chapter is a preliminary survey of some of those issues only.

Notes

[1]   Dominique Loh, "FPDA ministers want to set up disaster relief coordination centre", *Channel NewsAsia*, 5 June 2006, <www.channelnewsasia.com/stories/singaporelocalnews/view/212051/1/.html>.

2   Sebastian Rhodes Stampa, "The International Humanitarian Response System: Humanitarian and Civil Military Coordination", *Civil-Military Interaction Seminar*, Sydney, December 2009. Since then, the 2011 earthquake and subsequent tsunami centred near Japan are alone estimated to cost as much or more to recover from.

3   *International Strategy for Disaster Reduction, Hyogo Framework for Action 2005–2015: Building the Resilience of Nations and Communities to Disasters*, extract from the final report of the World Conference on Disaster Reduction, Kobe, Hygo, Japan, 18–22 January 2005, <www.unisdr.org/wcdr>.

4   John Twigg, "Disaster Risk Reduction: Mitigation and Preparedness in Development and Emergency Programming", *Good Practice Review*, Humanitarian Practice Network, Overseas Development Institute Number 9, March 2004, p. 320.

5   Sharon Wiharta et al., *The Effectiveness of Foreign Military Assets in Natural Disaster Response* (Stockholm: Stockholm International Peace Research Institute, 2008), p. 48.

6   Brian R. Selmeski, *Democracy, Economic Development and the Ecuadorian Armed Forces* (Brasilia: Center for Hemispheric Defense Studies, 2002).

7   Francisco Rey Marcos, "Military Participation in Humanitarian Action: Reflections on the Colombia case", *Humanitarian Exchange Magazine* 45 (December 2009) <www.odihpn.org/report.asp?id=3041>.

8   United Nations, Department of Humanitarian Affairs, "Guidelines on the Use of Foreign Military and Civil Defence Assets in Disaster Relief" (Oslo Guidelines), Project DPR 213/3 MCDA. May 1994, updated November 2006, rev 1.1 November 2007.

9   Ibid.

10 Asean Regional Forum, "Co-Chairs' Summary Report of the ARF Seminar on the Laws and Regulations on the Participation in International Disaster Relief by Armed Forces", Beijing, 22–25 April 2009, paragraph 6.

11 Ibid., paragraph 19.

12 Oxfam International, "OI Policy Compendium Note on the Provision of Aid by Military Forces", September 2007, p. 4.

13 Rajive Kohli, "Armed Forces in Disaster Risk Reduction" in *Disaster Risk Reduction in South Asia*, edited by Pardeep Sahni, Madhavi Ariyabandu (New Delhi: Prentice-Hall, 2003), p. 218.

14 Mark Pelling and Ailsa Holloway, *Legislation for Mainstreaming Disaster Risk Reduction* (Teddington, UK: Tearfund 2006).

15 Twigg, "Disaster Risk Reduction", op. cit., p. 75.

16 Non-Traditional Security Alert, "The Implementation of a Disaster Management Agreement in ASEAN: Towards Regional Preparedness?", Centre for Non-Traditional Security Studies, S. Rajaratnam School of International Studies, September 2010, Issue 2.

[17] Wayne Mapp, "Humanitarian and Disaster Relief in the Asia-Pacific", speech at the Shangri-La Dialogue, Singapore, 7 June 2010 <www.beehive. govt.nz/speech/humanitarian+and+disaster+relief+asia-pacific+shangri-la+dialogue>.

[18] United Nations Office for the Coordination of Humanitarian Affairs, Civil-Military Coordination Section, *Asia-Pacific Regional Guidelines for the Use of Foreign Military Assets in Natural Disaster Response Operations*, 5th APC-MADRO conference, Bangkok, Thailand, 14–15 October 2010.

[19] Ibid., paragraph 9.

[20] ASEAN, Chairman's Statement of the First ASEAN Defence Ministers' Meeting-Plus, "ADMM-Plus: Strategic Cooperation for Peace, Stability, and Development in the Region", Hanoi 12 October 2010 <www.aseansec.org/25352.htm>.

[21] Air Vice Marshal Kevin Paule, cited in Michael Weaver and Hugh McKenzie, "The Calm after a Storm", *Defence Magazine* (1) 2011, p. 20.

[22] We should note here that many NGOs have a number of these generic capabilities. For example, there are significant training programmes and great technical expertise within many NGOs. Few, if any, however, collect the range of capabilities within the same organizational structure.

[23] For more detail on potential problems surrounding the use of the armed forces in HA/DR see Evan A. Laksmana, "The Indonesian Defence Forces and Disaster Relief: Potential Pitfalls and Challenges", *RSIS Commentary*, No. 160/2010 (29 November 2010).

[24] United Nations Development Group, *Integrating Disaster Risk Reduction into the CCA and UNDAF: A Guide for UN Country Teams*, UNDG Guidance Note <www.undg.org/drr>.

[25] Note, "language" here can include the requirement not to use military jargon to interlocutors who do not use that jargon.

[26] Paul Dibb, "Conflict Must Remain the Clear Priority for ADF", *The Australian*, 17 June 2011.

7

A Quasi-Pact of Enduring Value: A Malaysian Perspective of the FPDA

Zakaria Ahmad

Far from being a mere relic of the Cold War,[1] the Five Power Defence Arrangements (FPDA), has survived four decades since its inception in 1971. It may be argued, as its principal protagonists do, that it has constantly been "re-tooled" to meet the changing challenges of Southeast Asia's security landscape. In the post-9/11 period, more importance has been accorded to the threat of terrorism, and more recently, to Non-Traditional Security (NTS) issues. However, the bulk of FPDA military exercises and the operation of Integrated Air Defence System (IADS) of Peninsular Malaysia and Singapore, now broadened to area defence, reflect more traditional security concerns.

The FPDA's Relevance and Durability

In assessing its present status and future direction, it is germane to consider the *raison d'etre* of the FPDA in relation to the central security concerns of its principal actors, namely Malaysia, Singapore and Australia. The other two members, Britain and New Zealand, are more "peripheral", albeit committed to the FPDA. Students of international security argue that since the end of the Cold War and the concomitant demise of bipolar rivalry between the United States and the former Soviet Union, the threat of military conflict and major inter-state war has diminished. In Southeast Asia, with the advent of the Association of Southeast Asian Nations (ASEAN) and its gradual transformation to encompass all ten of the region's states, the danger of inter-state war has also been deemed to be remote. In view of these factors, critics have postulated that the FPDA is an anachronism that should have met its demise, perhaps even in its early years.

That the FPDA has survived since 1971 is indicative of its relevance to its three principal actors. It is often overlooked that the FPDA was established at a time of great uncertainty, political turbulence and regional turmoil. For Southeast Asia, the period from the 1940s to the 1970s witnessed war, the tumult of decolonization and the assertion of nationalism of its newly-independent states which were confronted by issues of survival, development and communist uprisings.[2] In 1964–66, Malaysia and Singapore faced the phenomenon of *Konfrontasi* from Indonesia, bringing home the threat and reality of external military aggression. This historical experience suggests that Malaysia and Singapore are not unmindful of conventional military aggression that may engulf these two states in the future, as had happened in the past.

From another perspective, the survival of the FPDA may be the happy consequence of two not unrelated factors which may not have been in the minds of its signatories. First, that the FPDA has provided a vehicle that contributes to the non-inevitability, or perhaps the mitigation of the likelihood, of hostilities between Malaysia and Singapore; and, second, the continued presence and engagement, even after 40 years, of external military forces (principally from Australia, and to a lesser extent New Zealand and Britain) in Southeast Asia. Australia's role, in particular, is important because the FPDA is relevant to Canberra's strategic assessments and perceptions of the region (both Southeast Asia and the larger Asia-Pacific region) in relation to its own defence, and also because of its politico-military role in the FPDA, especially in the command and organization of the air defence of Peninsular Malaysia and Singapore.

An analysis of the FPDA's future would be more useful in terms of evaluating its role and efficacy and whether there is an enduring commitment from the member-states. Because it is an "Arrangements", the

FPDA approximates more a defence "quasi-pact", denoting a non-binding quality to its mode of operationalization. One may argue that the FPDA is made up of like-minded countries, with an abiding sense of unity in that they are members of the Commonwealth. This sense of unity has been underscored by the commitment of Britain, Australia and New Zealand to the defence and security of Malaysia and Singapore, beginning from the Second World War through the Malayan Emergency (1948–60) and the period of *Konfrontasi*. Indeed, from this historical perspective, the FPDA is but an extension of the Anglo-Malaysian Defence Agreement (AMDA) — although in a looser form — and a surrogate mechanism, as it were, when Britain terminated its military obligations East of Suez from 1971 onwards.

The FPDA and Non-Traditional Security

Some may argue that the future relevance of the FPDA may hinge on the challenges of NTS issues that have become more salient since the end of the Cold War, and efforts to get countries to embark on ventures such as Humanitarian Assistance and Disaster Relief (HA/DR). However, in general, it needs be noted that analyses of NTS challenges in the member countries are still on-going, and in Malaysia and Singapore have only begun to receive greater attention from policy-makers and scholars.[3] Therefore, observations on NTS issues in relation to the FPDA are still preliminary in nature.

A focus on NTS issues by a mechanism devised essentially to deal with traditional security may steer the FPDA in a procrustean fashion towards the belief that it is the only way to prolong its life beyond an otherwise defunct status. The idea of defunctness, however, based as it is on the assumption that conventional threats on which the FPDA was founded is no longer valid, is not shared by defence and security planners of at least its principal members.

It has been vigorously argued by NTS proponents that "a majority of challenges are transnational in nature with regard to their origins, conception and effects."[4] Further, NTS proponents acknowledge that "while the state is a primary referent, it encompasses other referent objects, such as human collectivities".[5] Thus, NTS "provides an alternative approach to security studies by examining the conditions experienced by individuals and communities, highlighting the threats and insecurities that they face".[6] Such an approach may be applicable to the FPDA insofar as NTS issues have begun to be discussed within policy circles. Starting first with discussions on asymmetric threats, the scope has been expanded to intelligence exchanges and concerns with smuggling, piracy, drugs, illegal fishing and the proliferation of weapons of mass destruction.[7]

However, neo-realists, perhaps even resurrected liberalist students of strategy, may view NTS challenges as marginal to the FPDA. Indeed there appears to be no consensual view in policy circles as to how the FPDA would approach NTS challenges in operational terms. According to one source, "some elements of NTS have been introduced, but the bulk of exercises still remain in the genre of joint and combined conventional warfare".[8] This source further notes that it would be difficult to conduct NTS exercises with other agencies alongside the armed forces of FPDA members.[9] Moreover, some NTS activities are already being conducted in other regional and sub-regional formats, as in coordinated air and naval patrols in the Straits of Malacca.

Two issue-areas that can potentially assume importance and receptivity in the FPDA are Military Operations Other Than War (MOOTW) and Peace Keeping Operations (PKO). Since the 26 December 2004 Indian Ocean Tsunami, there has been heightened understanding of the potential for the mobilization and utilization of militaries in HADR operations. However, it is not clear if there is agreement within the FPDA that such activities should be subsumed under, or added to, the current undertakings of the FPDA. That these two areas have not really become part of the FPDA agenda may be due to the reluctance on the part of the countries concerned because it could possibly entail complications in command and control in what will be a multilateral undertaking. Moreover, such undertakings will also call for greater commitment of resources, financial and otherwise, from the FPDA states.

Malaysia and the FPDA

Within Malaysia itself, especially in the defence and security community, there has been debate as to the efficacy and even the utility of the FPDA. There have also been some rumblings from military professionals that the FPDA air defence cover only extends down the spine of Peninsular Malaysia through Singapore, and that this is more beneficial to Singapore than to Malaysia.

There are still political issues that exist in the FPDA. Foremost is the notion of the "indivisibility" of the defence of Malaysia and Singapore which was a core tenet of the 1971 agreement. It is no longer believed, north of the causeway, that Malaysia's and Singapore's defence is inextricably linked — both have their sets of priorities and deal with very different needs and circumstances. The command of the IADS has always been held by an Australian; this is likely to continue until such time there is sufficient confidence that it can be held by either a Malaysian or a Singaporean. Similarly, land exercises on Malaysian soil with participation of the Singapore Armed Forces are still not possible because of "political sensitivities". It is highly unlikely that the FPDA will be expanded to include other members, or that its scope of air defence will be extended to Sabah and Sarawak, or that its scale of exercises will become much larger undertakings. There is "caution" in the progress of the FPDA; for the moment, Kuala Lumpur is comfortable with its gradual consolidation, its relatively low profile and its "soft" consultative character.

Yet it is important to note that the deterrence value of the FPDA is still appreciated. Also, FPDA exercises provide experience in command and control of combined operations, facilitate professionalism, training and interoperability and serve as an avenue for defence diplomacy. To be sure, there are limits and constraints, and the allocation of resources by the five powers in the event of the "real thing" (that is, an attack on Malaysia and Singapore) is still not a matter that is well understood. Still, over the past four decades, the FPDA has provided time and space for both Malaysia and Singapore to develop their military capabilities; today both countries have capable air forces with the requisite air power to defend the two countries so that the external partners of the FPDA need not be at the front or first line of air defence. In the maritime dimension, the annual exercises have enabled FPDA navies to work together in more sophisticated joint operations which include air and land elements. Also, IADS has now been expanded to include area defence as well. In all of these, it is more than apparent that Malaysia has benefited from being part of FPDA.

It should be noted that the value Malaysia places on the FPDA is based on a realistic appreciation of its own defence posture and capability and that it has been a key consideration in Kuala Lumpur's strategic planning. Even though the principal theme of Malaysia's defence policy is achieving "self-reliance",[10] implicit in this theme is the understanding that Malaysia can rely on external help from its friends and allies in the event of any contingency.

Questioning the value of the FPDA as a consultative arrangement on the grounds that in the event of an emergency, no defensive military action may be taken by the signatories, is tantamount to conjecture. It is akin to asking "What if deterrence fails?" But that a consultative process will be conducted in the FPDA should there be an attack or threat of attack on Malaysia and Singapore is at least an insurance and a deterrent (psychological or otherwise) to would-be aggressors.

Conclusion

In the final analysis, when viewed against the evolving security landscape of Southeast Asia and the Asia Pacific — which is characterized by uncertainties associated with shifts in the balance of power, the rise of China and India, and the changing priorities of the United States — the FPDA is regarded as yet another evolving part of the region's security architecture. Thus the FPDA does serve a purpose in an uncertain regional security environment, one that is better to have than be without, and which has provided a useful handle in allowing for Malaysia to build its own defence capacity. The FPDA has "remained relevant to its members, has held them together and there is sustained interest in maintaining the defence of Malaysia and Singapore against as external threat".[11] As a quasi-pact, the FPDA does contribute to a sense of national and regional security, and continues to be useful now, just as when it first came into being, and possibly in the future.

Notes

[1] Reference to the Cold War and its relevance to the FPDA is not a mere intellectual observation. In an interview with a former Chief of the Royal Malaysian Air Force, it was opined that the FPDA was an "instrumentality of the US to contain communist influence in Malaysia and Singapore", and that "it provided surveillance capabilities and information to the US".

[2] For a good account of this scenario, see P. Lyon, *War and Peace in Southeast Asia* (Oxford: Oxford University Press, 1969).

[3] Pioneering and excellent efforts in analyzing Non-Traditional Security issues have and are being conducted by the Centre for Non-Traditional Security (NTS) Studies of the S. Rajaratnam School of International Studies (RSIS) of the Nanyang Technological University, Singapore.

[4] *Studying Non-Traditional Security in Asia* edited by Ralf Emmers, Mely Caballero-Anthony and Amitav Acharya (Singapore: Michael Cavendish, 2006), xiv.

[5] Ibid.

[6] Ibid.

[7] See Mohd. Shaifuddin b. Mohd Shariff, "Five Power Defence Arrangements (FPDA) and Southeast Asia Security: A Study of Evolution", unpublished Master of Social Sciences (Defence Studies) thesis, Universiti Kebangsaan Malaysia, 2009, p. 28.

[8] Written response from a senior official, Ministry of Defence, Malaysia, 8 February 2011.

[9] Ibid.

[10] Ministry of Defence, *Pertahanan Malaysia: Ke – Arah Pertahanan Yang Berdirikari (Malaysian Defence – Towards Self-Reliance)* (Kuala Lumpur: Ministry of Defence, 1997). See also Ministry of Defence, *Dasar Pertahanan Negara (Natinal Defence Policy)* (Kuala Lumpur: Ministry of Defence, 2010).

[11] Shaifuddin, "Five Power Defence Arrangements", op. cit., pp. 77–79.

8

The FPDA and Asia's Changing Strategic Environment: A View from New Zealand

Mark G. Rolls

As we mark the 40th anniversary of the Five Power Defence Arrangements (FPDA) — which have been variously described as "an obligation to consult", a "minilateral defence coalition", and even an "alliance"[1] — and attempt to assess its place in Asia's changing strategic environment, it is worth beginning with the provision of some historical context. This will be attempted through a brief overview of New Zealand's attitudes towards the FPDA and the place which it has occupied in New Zealand's defence policy and approach to regional security during the Arrangements' lifetime. The main features of the current and likely future strategic environment, as they are perceived by New Zealand, will then be outlined through an examination of the recently released Defence White Paper. The FPDA's role in this strategic environment will subsequently be analysed before the chapter concludes with an assessment of whether or not it has continued utility in that environment and what its place is (if any) in the regional security architecture.

In advance of a meeting of the five powers in June 1968, the Cabinet had decided that New Zealand needed to "avoid any commitments of a long-term or specific nature and discourage any disposition on the part of Malaysia and Singapore to look to Australia and New Zealand to pull their chestnuts out of the fire".[2] This evident desire to avoid over commitment was also readily apparent in the wake of the April 1971 meeting of the five countries' prime ministers at which they agreed to the eventual replacement of the Anglo-Malayan Defence Agreement with the FPDA. That the Arrangements were to be no more than a commitment to consult was emphatically stated by New Zealand's Prime Minister, Keith Holyoake.[3]

After a decade of operation, and at a time when efforts were underway to revitalize the FPDA, a distinct lack of enthusiasm was also apparent; at least as far as the Ministry of Foreign Affairs was concerned. The Ministry, Jim Rolfe notes, viewed the Arrangements as an anachronism, established "in different times, essentially as a transitional measure following British withdrawal East of Suez. We do not see that New Zealand has anything to gain by a revitalization of the FPDA".[4] The perception of the FPDA in the Ministry of Defence, perhaps not surprisingly, was rather different. Here, value was to be found for New Zealand in the "networking and training aspects of the Arrangements and [the Ministry] could see no merit in questioning a relationship which had worked for some ten years."[5]

Although in the early 1980s Defence avoided questioning the utility of the FPDA, and the February 1987 White Paper — *The Defence of New Zealand* — included the FPDA among New Zealand's interests, in reality the focus was now almost entirely on "[New Zealand's] immediate region."[6] Indeed, the areas of "direct strategic concern" identified were New Zealand, Australia and Antarctica.[7] Such thinking, along with a traditional desire to avoid expensive military commitments, provided the context for the announcement by Prime Minister David Lange in December 1986 that the New Zealand infantry battalion in Singapore would be withdrawn before the end of 1989. Lange contended, however, that the withdrawal would not affect New Zealand's participation in the FPDA.[8]

A decade after *The Defence of New Zealand* was released, and against the backdrop of a major emphasis by the National-led government on the importance to New Zealand of East Asia, *The Shape of New Zealand Defence: A White Paper* was released. This reiterated that one of the "principal elements" of New Zealand defence policy was "contributing to regional security" and that this included "maintaining ... key defence relationships with Australia and our Five Power Defence Arrangements (FPDA) partners".[9] The 1997 White Paper went on to state that: "The continued stability of South-East Asia is one of ... [New Zealand's] most important security goals .... second only to the common security of Australia and New Zealand."[10] Due acknowledgement was made of the efforts by Malaysia and Singapore in the 1990s to adapt the FPDA so as to ensure its continued relevance and it was stated that the FPDA was "important for New Zealand not just as our only formal security link with the region, but because of the value the NZDF [New Zealand Defence Force] gains from FPDA exercises and other military exchanges."[11]

The desire to contribute to regional security — and by association the continuing commitment to, and importance of, the FPDA — can be seen as part of the National-led government's attempts to demonstrate that its interest in Asia was motivated by more than purely economic self-interest. Defence cooperation, therefore, was part of New Zealand's wider engagement with East Asia.

A rather different approach, Robert Ayson contends, was evident during the first year in office of the Labour-led Government which was elected in October 1999. "The 1999–2000 period did much to delink the defence role from New Zealand's overall approach to East Asia. One symbolic representation of this change was the disappearance of the old argument ... that Southeast Asia could be viewed as something of a land-bridge to Australia and New Zealand."[12] While the government still paid "homage" to the Arrangements and indicated that it would "live up to New Zealand's obligations" under them, it also "suggested that New Zealand was not an advocate of alliance-based approaches to regional security management."[13] The clear preference in fact was for participation in multilateral regional institutions such as the ASEAN Regional Forum (ARF).

Irrespective of the new government's intentions to uphold New Zealand's obligations under the FPDA, the country's ability to contribute effectively to the FPDA's increasingly sophisticated combined exercise programme was seriously constrained by the decision to disband the Royal New Zealand Air Force's (RNZAF) air combat wing — based on two squadrons of A-4K Skyhawks — by the end of December 2001.[14]

The increased importance attached to non-traditional security issues in the wake of the end of the Cold War and the terrorist attacks of 11 September 2001 (which had a marked effect on the evolution of the FPDA itself),[15] was not lost on the New Zealand Government. Indeed, for the government, the significance of these issues was such that it "suggest[ed] the possibility of new elements of a security relationship — even a defence relationship — with a number of East Asian countries."[16] As a consequence, there was support from New Zealand for "expanding the remit of the FPDA to cover responses to non-traditional maritime security challenges."[17]

The fact that New Zealand had a range of interests in Asia, and thus a stake in the maintenance of regional security and stability, was clearly acknowledged in the Ministry of Foreign Affairs and Trade's *Our Future With Asia* which was published in 2007. It was certainly recognized that New Zealand should deepen its defence and security understanding of the region and that, overall, Wellington needed to be more active in engaging with the region. The role of the NZDF's contribution to the furtherance of peace and security was acknowledged, and New Zealand was described as "an active participant in the Five Power Defence Arrangements."[18] The language used to describe New Zealand's association with the FPDA thus taking on a more dynamic tone.

It was now apparent that there was something of a convergence of views between Foreign Affairs and Defence (or should one say a more "whole of government" approach, the term currently in vogue). Prior to the publication of the *Defence White Paper 2010*, the FPDA featured prominently in the Ministry of Defence's description of New Zealand's multilateral defence engagement with Southeast Asia. In noting that participating in multilateral military exercises represents "a key component of New Zealand's defence interaction" in the region, the FPDA was regarded as particularly important in this respect. Moreover, as the FPDA has begun to enhance capacity-building in non-traditional areas such as maritime security and Humanitarian Assistance and Disaster Relief (HA/DR), it "remains a relevant and important part of New Zealand's approach to security in our region."[19]

The *Defence White Paper 2010* very clearly states the significance of the FPDA to New Zealand: "New Zealand's security relationships with Singapore and Malaysia, founded on the FPDA, are likely to remain our most enduring in the region. So long as these regional states maintain their support for the FPDA then New Zealand will continue to do so. As New Zealand's most significant operational security link to Southeast Asia, the FPDA will continue to provide a valuable anchor for the presence of our defence assets in the region."[20] In addition to providing this operational security link, New Zealand's participation in the FPDA is viewed as one way in which it can contribute to the maintenance of peace and security in the wider East Asian strategic environment and be seen to be doing so. As the White Paper puts it, New Zealand's "interests are best served by a region in which all countries and especially the major powers agree on the importance of stability and prosperity, and share a common understanding of how these goals should be secured. We contribute to that stability and prosperity, including by working alongside partners and friends in structures such as the FPDA, the ASEAN Regional Forum, and the ASEAN Defence Ministers' Meeting-Plus."[21]

Although in terms of New Zealand's strategic outlook up to 2035 the White Paper regards it as "highly unlikely" that New Zealand will face a "direct military threat", it is readily acknowledged that "the next 25 years are likely to be more challenging than the 25 years just past."[22] Indeed, the main "theme … is that of an increasingly uncertain strategic outlook."[23] Within an overarching strategic context in which "the underlying stability and predictability which has characterised international relations since at least the end of the Cold War is now being tested",[24] three particular concerns are identified: shifts in economic power; the narrowing of the military advantage gap (including the fact that an increasing number of states will have access to weapons of mass destruction); and the various challenges posed by weak states and the related problem of terrorism.[25]

Following on from the identification of international (or system) level concerns, the White Paper goes on to identify those which are specific to East Asia. It does this through an assessment of Southeast Asia and Northeast Asia respectively. In terms of the former, and after noting the significant military modernization which has been enabled by economic growth, the principal security challenges are identified as "Islamist and other forms of terrorism, weapons proliferation, and piracy". The existence of inter-ASEAN tensions, and those within some of the ASEAN states themselves, is also noted.[26]

In Northeast Asia the strategic environment is perceived as more challenging in many ways because it is characterized by shifts in the "strategic balance" itself. While it is acknowledged that China gains from, and contributes to, stability and prosperity in the region, New Zealand perceives that "there will be a natural tendency for it to define and pursue its interests in a more forthright way on the back of growing wealth and power". The speed with which China is modernizing its armed forces and developing power projection capabilities, and the reaction that this might generate from its neighbours, could "test the relationships of the major regional powers".[27] Tensions surrounding the situation on the Korean Peninsula, Taiwan, and the South China Sea disputes are viewed as likely to continue. They will be "fuelled by multiple protagonists", some of whom are "unpredictable". The outbreak of conflict in any of these areas, it hardly needs stating, "would have a serious impact on security and confidence in the wider region".[28]

Common to both sub-regions, and listed under the sub-heading of open trade routes, are the issues of maritime security and piracy (which is obviously a global concern too). In terms of the former, it is recognized that the existence of territorial disputes will lead to "parts of maritime Asia … remain[ing] a contested space over the next 25 years and this could potentially be expressed militarily". A combination of "resource competition and narrowly defined national interest" will be "a volatile mix". With regard to piracy, it is thought that this problem will continue to exist even "in well-regulated spaces such as the Straits of Malacca".[29]

From this overview of the strategic outlook contained in the *Defence White Paper 2010*, it is readily apparent that from New Zealand's perspective there are likely to be elements of continuity and change in the East Asian strategic environment over the next 25 years. There would be little here that would be disagreed with, or disputed, by New Zealand's FPDA partners.

The most significant element of change, which would again be uncontroversial, is the recognition that to some extent the power balance is shifting. Indeed, concern about major power rivalry, and how best to moderate it, has been a recent feature of the IISS Asia Security Summit (the Shangri-La Dialogue) and Track II meetings such as the ASEAN-Australia-New Zealand Trilateral Dialogue. The ability of smaller states to moderate this rivalry is, of course, severely limited. Their efforts are largely confined to attempts to "enmesh" the Great Powers in the existing regional multilateral institutions and, by so doing, help to develop a "sense of security interdependence" between them and organizations such as ASEAN and regional states such as New Zealand.[30] Clearly the FPDA has no role to play in this regard, or with respect to the Korean Peninsula and Taiwan for that matter, but it has been argued that for New Zealand a potentially competitive strategic environment only increases the appeal of traditional linkages such as the FPDA.[31]

This appeal, it can be argued, does not just apply to New Zealand: it applies equally, if not more so, to Malaysia and Singapore. These two states do not face the same pressures as they did when the FPDA was established 40 years ago; there is a reduced prospect of major inter-state conflict in the region; and the defence capabilities of both states have increased considerably. However, in an uncertain, unpredictable and potentially competitive strategic environment in which military modernization is occurring, then the traditional focus of the FPDA — the defence of Malaysia and Singapore from external aggression — still has utility. The long-standing idea, noted by many commentators, that the FPDA performs a psychological deterrence function,[32] has continuing relevance. Indeed, Malaysia and Singapore still see the FPDA as having an important deterrent effect.[33]

Moreover, in practical terms, the FPDA continues to play a useful role in the enhancement of the military capabilities of both states. Efforts to increase the FPDA's capacity for joint and combined activity were initiated over a decade ago with the approval by the FPDA Defence Ministers of *The Future of the FPDA Operational Arrangements — Version 10* paper in 2000. Capacity-building and moves to increase interoperability have occurred through an increasingly sophisticated combined exercise programme along with expanded opportunities for professional development. These aspects of the workings of the FPDA are obviously of benefit to the NZDF too. Although there is no intention to actually develop a real joint operational capability — even in the area of air defence (the FPDA's principal area of concern)[34] — such moves can be expected to continue. They may, however, be subject to the constraints placed on the various members as a result of operational commitments elsewhere in the world or cutbacks in defence expenditure.

It is also worth noting that the training and exercise programmes which occur under the auspices of the Arrangements, and which have fashioned a habit of cooperation among the armed forces of the five powers over a long period of time, often have utility beyond the FPDA area. In Afghanistan, the armed forces of Malaysia and Singapore operate in tandem with those from Australia and New Zealand in preference to the forces deployed by any other country. Indeed, Malaysia and Singapore have both indicated that it was the degree of familiarity and comfort built up over many years of FPDA association and activity which influenced their decision.[35]

One of the features of the current and future strategic environment envisaged by the *Defence White Paper 2010*, as we have seen, was the increased significance which would be attached to non-traditional security (NTS) issues. Some of those which the White Paper highlights included Islamist and other types of terrorism; weak states; maritime security; piracy; and the proliferation of weapons of mass destruction (WMD). There are many more non-traditional security issues, of course.[36] The introduction of non-traditional issues into the regional strategic environment, and the FPDA's recognition of this and response to it, has been widely noted. The FPDA is not alone in this of course: ASEAN, the ARF, and the ASEAN Defence Ministers' Meeting (ADMM), have responded too.[37] Moves by the FPDA to respond to this changed strategic environment were apparent with the approval of *The Future Role and Development of the FPDA* by the FPDA Defence Ministers in 2004 and the subsequent drawing up of *The Roadmap to Implement the FPDA Defence Ministers Non-Conventional Capacity Guidance*.

Among the various NTS issues considered, it was determined that priority should be accorded to maritime security (which is of considerable interest to New Zealand) and the FPDA's exercise programme has been amended and expanded accordingly to include non-traditional maritime threats. Again, as was the case in the conventional arena, the intention is not to develop a joint FPDA capability, but to improve the ability of the members to operate with each other. This would certainly be of benefit too in the event they should be tasked with working alongside each other in operations of this type outside the FPDA area.[38]

Although at the FPDA informal Defence Ministers' Meeting in June 2004 it was announced that regular exchanges of intelligence on terrorism and transnational threats such as piracy, illegal fishing, and the proliferation of WMD would be initiated, this has not really occurred beyond the exchange of information as part of the normal planning process for FPDA exercises. The protocols surrounding the exchange of classified material make it too difficult to do this in practice. The exchange of intelligence on maritime security issues such as illegal fishing, smuggling and transnational crime occurs instead through Singapore's Changi C2 Centre in which all five members either have personnel stationed or have access to.[39] The ability of the FPDA to enhance its members' capability to respond to some NTS threats (primarily those pertaining to aspects of maritime security) is, therefore, apparent too although in the area of terrorism and WMD this is limited or non-existent.

A final aspect of the current and perceived future strategic environment to which the FPDA has responded, and in which it has a role to play, is the recognition of the region's susceptibility to natural disasters and the devastating effects these can have. Natural disasters, and the attendant need to develop effective capabilities for HA/DR, have long been regarded as an important NTS issue. Many ASEAN states have incorporated the need to respond to these in their defence planning and in recent years HA/DR has featured prominently on the ASEAN and ASEAN-led non-traditional regional security agenda.[40]

In the wake of the 2004 Indian Ocean Tsunami, and cognizant of moves by other organizations, the FPDA Defence Ministers decided at their meeting in 2006 that the FPDA should consider how cooperation in the area of HA/DR could be furthered. A paper on this — *Building Capacity in Humanitarian and Disaster Relief*— was drawn up the same year and in 2007 the FPDA developed a *Roadmap of Activities to Build FPDA HADR Capacity*.[41] The intention, as was the case with maritime security, is not to create a joint FPDA HA/DR operational capability. Rather, it is to increase the interoperability of the FPDA members' armed forces for HA/DR operations in the event that their forces should be conducting these in one place at the same time.[42] Again, this could be outside the FPDA area. The FPDA will continue to pursue capacity-building by following and, at some stage, updating its HA/DR roadmap. New Zealand, which has long recognized the role which the NZDF has to play in HA/DR operations at home and in the South Pacific and further afield, is both welcoming and supportive of such moves by the FPDA.[43]

Lying at the heart of the FPDA's efforts to respond to the changing regional strategic environment is undoubtedly an attempt to ensure both its continued relevance in that environment and its continued utility to the members themselves in terms of the capabilities which they want their armed forces to have. The moves to promote capacity-building in the areas of non-traditional security and HA/DR can certainly be seen in this light. That the FPDA is as much about providing benefits to its members as it is about contributing to the regional security architecture is often overlooked when attempts are made to assess whether or not it has a future.

When the question of whether or not the FPDA has a future has been discussed in recent years, attention has always been drawn to the fact that it complements other institutions and initiatives to promote regional security and that it is the only multilateral organization with an operational dimension.[44] The emergence of functional groupings such as the Malacca

Straits Patrols and, especially, the initiation of ADMM-Plus might, therefore, lead to the idea that the FPDA could perhaps be supplanted. This is not a view which is held in New Zealand, however. Indeed, from the New Zealand perspective the FPDA will continue to serve a particular purpose which would not be accomplished by a broader grouping, especially ADMM Plus, and would not encompass a permanent function over and above defending Malaysia and Singapore.[45]

Although the *Defence White Paper 2010* notes the importance of the FPDA to New Zealand, it does not mention the importance of the Arrangements themselves in the regional security architecture. The importance which New Zealand attaches to it, however, is implicit in the fact that it is given such emphasis in the White Paper and is clearly valued by New Zealand.[46] For New Zealand, the FPDA fits very nicely into one of the multiple layers in the regional security architecture identified by Singapore's Defence Minister Teo Chee Hean. It should, therefore, be seen as one of those "practical forms of defence cooperation among countries, such as military exercises and exchanges, [which] complement the role of dialogue in advancing transparency, reducing the chances of misunderstanding or miscalculation, and building confidence and trust in each other."[47]

For the foreseeable future then, the FPDA will continue to perform its original role of contributing to the defence of Malaysia and Singapore; help its members develop capacity in a range of new areas (particularly maritime security and HA/DR); and make a contribution, albeit limited, to the regional security architecture. Realistically, it cannot, and should not, be expected to play any wider role in the current and future regional strategic environment.

Notes

[1]   In discussing the replacement of AMDA with the FPDA, Michael Leifer contended that "an obligation to consult in the event of any form of external attack was substituted for the automatic commitment to respond" which the former had contained. Michael Leifer, *Dictionary of the Modern Politics of South East Asia* (London: Routledge, 1995), p. 95. The term "minilateral defence coalition" is that employed by Ralph Emmers. Ralph Emmers, "The Role of the Five Power Defence Arrangements in the Southeast Asian Security Architecture", *RSIS Working Paper*, no. 195 (April 2010): 2. It is Jim Rolfe's contention that the "FPDA is ... clearly an alliance in the generally accepted sense

that an alliance is a grouping of states between which there is an expectation of military action or the consideration of military action if the situation with **any** [emphasis added] of the partners warrants it." Jim Rolfe, "Anachronistic Past or Positive Future: New Zealand and the Five Power Defence Arrangements", *CSS Working Paper*, 4/95, fn. 13, p. 27. This description of the FPDA would seem questionable, though, since there would be no expectation of either of these things in the event of any situation concerning the UK, Australia or New Zealand. It is Carlyle Thayer's contention that the FPDA "was merely a consultative forum, not a formal alliance". Carlyle Thayer, "The Five Power Defence Arrangements: The Quiet Achiever", *Security Challenges* 3, no. 1 (February 2007): 79. An Australian article on the FPDA also states that: "The FPDA is not an alliance". Kate Boswood, "Engaging our interests: the Five Power Defence Arrangements and its contribution to regional security", <http://www.defence.gov.au/defencemagazine/editions/200708_09/isip_fivepower.pdf >.

2   Malcolm McKinnon, *Independence and Foreign Policy: New Zealand in the World Since 1935* (Auckland: Auckland University Press, 1993), p. 169.

3   Ibid., p. 171.

4   Ministry of Foreign Affairs brief for the Prime Minister, "Visit by the Prime Minister to Europe, April 1988: Five Power Defence Arrangements", April 1988, on file 03440/3, *FPDA*, cited Rolfe, "Anachronistic Past or Positive Future", op. cit., p. 8.

5   Rolfe, "Anachronistic Past or Positive Future", op. cit., p. 8.

6   Mark G. Rolls, "Growing Apart: New Zealand and Malaysia", in *Southeast Asia and New Zealand* edited by Anthony L. Smith (Singapore and Wellington: Institute of Southeast Asian Studies/NZIIA and Victoria University Press, 2005), p. 236.

7   *New Zealand Foreign Affairs Review* 37, no. 2 (January–March 1987): 15.

8   Rolls, "Growing Apart", op. cit., p. 236.

9   *The Shape of New Zealand's Defence: A White Paper* (Wellington: Ministry of Defence, 1997), p. 7.

10 Ibid., p. 17. South-East Asia's significance is noted because it is "the only land bridge through which Australia and New Zealand could be threatened". Ibid.

11 Ibid.

12 Robert Ayson, "New Zealand and East Asia's Security Future", *Outlook 03* (April 2006): 8.

13 Ibid.

14 This decision received criticism from some quarters in Malaysia and Singapore at the time and has subsequently been referred to on occasion in Track II meetings.

15 See, for example, Damon Bristow, "The FPDA: Southeast Asia's Unknown

Regional Security Organisation", *Contemporary Southeast Asia* 27, no. 1 (April
2005); and Andrew T. H. Tan, "The Five Power Defence Arrangements: The
Continuing Relevance", *Contemporary Security Policy* 29, no. 2 (August 2008).

16   Ayson, "New Zealand and East Asia's Security Future", op. cit., p. 8.
17   Ibid.
18   *Our Future With Asia* (Wellington: Ministry of Foreign Affairs and Trade, 2007),
     p. 23.
19   *New Zealand's Defence Engagement with Southeast Asia*, International Defence
     Relations Branch, Ministry of Defence, December 2009.
20   *Defence White Paper 2010* (Wellington: Ministry of Defence, November 2010),
     p. 30. For one Australian academic, however, the FPDA is not so much an
     "anchor" for New Zealand as a "toehold". Thayer, "The Quiet Achiever",
     op. cit., p. 94.
21   *Defence White Paper 2010*, p. 19.
22   Ibid., p. 10.
23   Ibid., p. 23.
24   Ibid.
25   See Ibid., pp. 24–25.
26   Ibid., p. 30.
27   Ibid.
28   Ibid.
29   Ibid., p. 32.
30   Mark G. Rolls, "Session II: The Role of ASEAN, Australia and New Zealand
     in Strengthening Regional Security", *AANZ Trilateral Dialogue, Kuala Lumpur,
     Malaysia, 5–6 December 2008*, <www.asianz.org>.
31   Ayson, "New Zealand and East Asia's Security Future", op. cit., p. 10.
32   See Emmers, "The Role of the Five Power Defence Arrangements", op. cit.,
     p. 8.
33   This point has also been made in recent years by both Damon Bristow and
     Carlyle Thayer. See Bristow, "The FPDA", op. cit., p. 11 and Thayer, "The Quiet
     Achiever", op. cit., p. 92.
34   Email correspondence with an official from the Ministry of Defence, Wellington,
     February, 2011.
35   Email correspondence with an official from the Ministry of Defence, Wellington,
     February, 2011. This official drew attention to the fact that the FPDA's role in
     developing the conventional capabilities of both Malaysia and Singapore's
     armed forces is also apparent in their ability to participate in multilateral
     operations such as those aimed at countering piracy off the Somali coast.
36   The list of non-traditional security issues is very extensive and can also include
     transnational crime; human trafficking; infectious diseases; and environmental
     degradation. For a discussion of those issues on the regional security agenda see

Mark G. Rolls, "ASEAN and the Non-Traditional Regional Security Agenda", *Track II India-New Zealand Dialogue, Wellington, New Zealand — 13–14 September 2010*, <www.asianz.org.nz>.

[37] Ibid.

[38] Email correspondence with an official from the Ministry of Defence, Wellington, February, 2011.

[39] Ibid.

[40] Rolls, "ASEAN and the Non-Traditional Regional Security Agenda", op. cit.

[41] Ibid.

[42] Email correspondence with an official from the Ministry of Defence, Wellington, February 2011.

[43] The *Defence White Paper 2010* lists one of the eight principal tasks the NZDF is expected to have the ability to conduct over the next 25 years as being "to contribute to whole-of-government efforts at home and abroad in resource protection, disaster relief, and humanitarian assistance". *Defence White Paper 2010*, p. 37. The NZDF's ability to contribute to such efforts has been ably demonstrated in the wake of the destructive February 2011 earthquake in Christchurch. The earthquake response also demonstrated the strength of the ties which New Zealand has with the Singapore Armed Forces (SAF), which has partly been developed through cooperation under the auspices of the FPDA. An SAF contingent which had just arrived in New Zealand for bilateral exercises provided valuable assistance in the aftermath of the earthquake, including participating in the cordons surrounding the badly damaged parts of the central city.

[44] See Emmers, "The Role of the Five Power Defence Arrangements", op. cit., p. 2 and Tan, "The Five Power Defence Arrangements", op. cit., p. 296.

[45] Email correspondence with an official from the Ministry of Defence, Wellington, February 2011.

[46] Ibid.

[47] Teo Chee Hean, Deputy Prime Minister and Minister for Defence, Singapore. The 9th IISS Asia Security Summit. The Shangri-la Dialogue. Sixth Plenary Session Renewing the Regional Security Architecture. 6 June 2010.

9

The Future of the FPDA in an Evolving Regional Strategic Environment

Tim Huxley

The Five Power Defence Arrangements (FPDA) is an oft-overlooked regional security institution. It is a curious security device in the sense that it embodies several paradoxes. The FPDA's most important roles are not those which are usually discussed openly. The most important non-regional player in the FPDA is not necessarily the one which plays the more prominent role in terms of its conventional military commitment. And while the FPDA is apparently anachronistic, in reality it continues to serve vital security roles, and this is likely to continue in the future.

To expand on the first of these paradoxes: it is sometimes said that the FPDA is a Cold War leftover that is irrelevant to the current and future security concerns of regional states. However, this argument misses the point that, although the FPDA was created during the Cold War in the context of the United Kingdom's (UK) military withdrawal from Southeast Asia in the late 1960s and early 1970s, its key roles were never related only to the Cold War. The five powers involved have always held diverse motives for participating in the FPDA. However, discussion of two of the FPDA's core rationales has always been essentially taboo.

The first of these implicit roles has been for the FPDA to act as a hedge against the resurgence of an unstable and threatening Indonesia which might endanger the security of Malaysia and Singapore, and perhaps also the wider sub-regional balance of power to the detriment of Australia, New Zealand and perhaps even the UK. While this has not been a realistic or immediate prospect since the FPDA was established in 1971, the ouster of President Soeharto in 1998, and the ensuing instability in Indonesia over the next three to four years, may have reminded FPDA members — and particularly Malaysia and Singapore — of the origins of the Arrangements in the wake of Jakarta's *Konfrontasi* of 1963–66. And while Indonesia's trajectory in terms of domestic stability and its willingness to play a constructive role regionally and internationally has seemed encouraging under the leadership of President Susilo Bambang Yudhoyono, there remain disquieting domestic political trends that could lead to the world's fourth most populous country becoming a less congenial neighbour in the future.

The FPDA's second implicit role has been to maintain essential channels of communication on defence and military matters between Malaysia and Singapore, and to build strategic confidence between the two Southeast Asian states whose sporadic mutual distrust sometimes highlights underlying existential tensions. It is widely-known that political issues deriving from these tensions have sometimes seriously disrupted bilateral defence relations between Malaysia and Singapore, leaving the FPDA as the main link between the two states' armed forces. Neither of these FPDA roles can be discussed openly in Southeast Asia, for fear of further undermining perennially neuralgic and sometimes strained relations within the Indonesia-Malaysia-Singapore triangle.

Nevertheless, in recent years the FPDA has displayed considerable flexibility in terms of the scope of its security ambit, notably adapting its exercise series in response to strategic concerns *du jour*, such as terrorism and Humanitarian Assistance and Disaster Relief. These exercises have doubtless helped to build a degree of interoperability between the forces of FPDA members, which has sometimes proved useful operationally outside the FPDA context. This was certainly true in the Australian-led intervention and security presence in East Timor from 1999: ultimately, forces from all

FPDA member-states were deployed in the territory. Familiarity deriving from FPDA contacts may also have helped some FPDA member-states' armies to operate alongside each other in Afghanistan.

Turning to the second paradox, it is clearly Australia that has played the most active role among the three extra-regional FPDA participants, diplomatically as well as in terms of its contribution of forces to FPDA exercises. The UK has never contributed either diplomatic enthusiasm or forces to the FPDA on the scale of Australia. The Conservative-Liberal Democrat coalition government's 2010 *Strategic Defence and Security Review* has further undermined Britain's capacity to project expeditionary military power, whether for real operational contingencies or for exercises. However, successive UK governments' commitment to perpetuating the country's status as one of five permanent UN Security Council members, and as a nuclear-weapons state maintaining a powerful and effectively invulnerable second-strike capability, is often overlooked in Asia. There can be little doubt that the UK's continuing involvement in the FPDA, which notably survived the *Strategic Defence and Security Review*, is significant for its FPDA partners and for other regional states in terms of Britain's continuing diplomatic and strategic weight.

One of the most frequently-heard comments about the FPDA is that it is "out-dated". Putting aside its possible continuing relevance in relation to developments in the immediate vicinity of Malaysia and Singapore, the changing strategic environment in the wider Asia-Pacific region suggests a range of adverse future scenarios in which membership of the FPDA could valuably supplement member states' other external security arrangements. All the signs in recent years suggest that the Asia-Pacific region's strategic environment will be characterised by the following major features. First, the distribution of power will undergo major shifts as the strategic weight of China increases (India seems less certain) and that of the United States undergoes decline in relative and perhaps absolute terms. Second, there will remain important potential flashpoints for state-on-state conflict, including the Taiwan Straits, the Korean Peninsula and the waters around China including the South China Sea. Third, there is increased likelihood of conflict over scarce resources, particularly maritime resources such as oil, gas and fish. Fourth, climate-change will have largely unpredictable security ramifications, but is likely to increase pressure on and further undermine already fragile states. Fifth, in the likely context of growing national disposable income, as well as the preceding points, defence policies and military capability build-ups are likely to become increasingly competitive — in other words, arms-racing, in which offensive military capabilities proliferate, is a real danger. Sixth, multilateral regional security institutions will remain weak and will continue to lack the capacity to mitigate regional tensions and conflict significantly. And finally, formal alliances may be out of fashion, but constructing tentative security relations on a mini-lateral basis will become even more common.

Against this backdrop, the FPDA — with its mix of regional and extra-regional member-states, lack of formal alliance commitments and proven adaptability— hardly seems anachronistic but, on the contrary, particularly well-suited to the strategic circumstances that seem likely to prevail in the future. The FPDA is a non-provocative form of hedging and confidence-building, and it would be surprising if any of the participating member-states chose to discard their FPDA commitments or role.

Index

www.ingramcontent.com/pod-product-compliance
Lightning Source LLC
Chambersburg PA
CBHW060344100426

42812CB00003B/1121